Editor: Catherine Bradley
Designer: Malcolm Smythe
Researcher: Cecilia Weston-Baker

Illustrated by: Peter Bull
and Amy Godfrey-Smythe

© Aladdin Books Ltd 1987

Designed and produced by
Aladdin Books Ltd
70 Old Compton Street
London W1V 5PA

First published in the
United States in 1988 by
Franklin Watts
387 Park Avenue South
New York, NY 10016

ISBN 0-531-10539-3

Library of Congress Catalog
Card Number: 87-51283

Printed in Belgium

CONFLICT IN THE 20TH CENTURY

THE MIDDLE EAST

CHARLES MESSENGER

Edited by Dr John Pimlott

FRANKLIN WATTS

New York · London · Toronto · Sydney

INTRODUCTION

In this volume, we turn to one of the most volatile and dangerous regions of the modern world – the Middle East. Of crucial importance because of its position and its oil, it has long suffered the attention of outside powers, while internally it has been riven by ethnic, religious and political divisions. Since the 1960s, the two rival superpowers – the United States and Soviet Union – have become increasingly involved.

Conflict in the region has taken many forms, but has centered on three major themes. First, there has been a persistent demand for national self-determination, initially against the Turks, then against the European colonial powers who replaced them in the aftermath of the First World War and finally against the independent countries which now make up the Middle East. In all cases, violence has resulted, often taking the form of guerrilla warfare or, more recently, terrorism.

The use of terror has come to be particularly associated with the Palestinians, and this highlights the second of the major themes: the emergence of Israel and Arab opposition to its existence. This has led to a succession of wars, many of which have developed into full-scale conflicts using tanks, aircraft and new technology provided by the superpowers.

The third theme is that of religious splits within the Muslim world. By the late 1980s, the spread of fundamentalism from Iran had helped to fuel the continuing violence in Lebanon and had led to a bitter, seemingly endless war in the Gulf between Iran and Iraq. The latter conflict, drawing in outside powers because of the threat to supplies of oil, had all the potential of a global crisis.

But there is hope. Efforts to gain peace, especially between Israel and the Arab powers, have enjoyed some success and are still being pursued. At the same time, both superpowers have shown that they are aware of the consequences of crises in the Middle East and know how far they can safely go. The only problem is, of course, that none of this helps to relieve the pressure in the region itself, where conflict and violence have become deep-rooted. In this respect, the picture remains a bleak one.

DR JOHN PIMLOTT *Series Editor*

EDITORIAL PANEL

Series Editor:
Dr John Pimlott, Senior Lecturer in the Department of War Studies and International Affairs, RMA Sandhurst, UK

Editorial Advisory Panel:
Brigadier General James L Collins Jr, US Army Chief of Military History 1970-82

General Sir John Hackett, former Commander-in-Chief of the British Army of the Rhine and Principal of King's College, London, UK

Ian Hogg, retired Master Gunner of the Artillery, British Army, and editor of *Jane's Infantry Weapons*

John Keegan, former Senior Lecturer in the Department of War Studies and International Affairs, RMA Sandhurst, UK, now Defense Correspondent, *Daily Telegraph*

Professor Laurence Martin, Vice-Chancellor of the University of Newcastle-upon-Tyne, UK

The author: Charles Messenger retired from the British Army in 1980 to become a full-time military writer after 21 years' service in the Royal Tank Regiment. He has written a number of books and articles on defense and historical affairs.

Burning the Shah's picture, Iran, 1978. A resurgence of Islamic fundamentalism led to the collapse of the Shah's attempt to create a modern, superstate in Iran. The Shah left the country in early 1979 and died shortly after in exile in Egypt.

CONTENTS

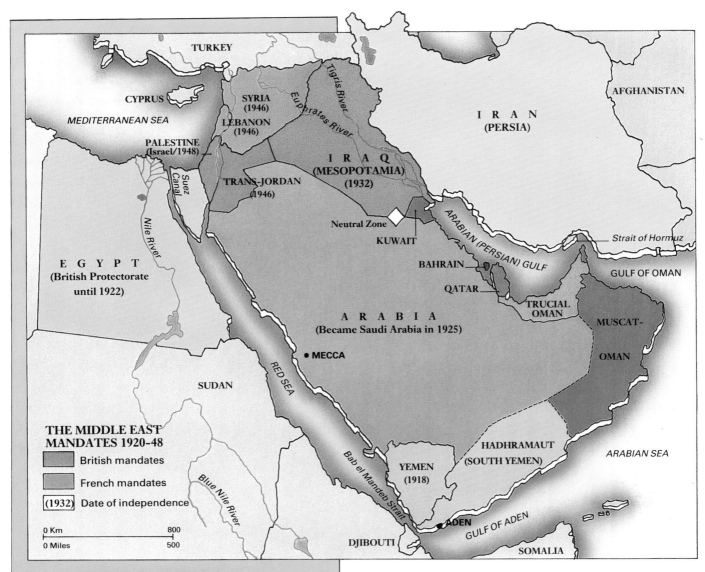

THE MIDDLE EAST
MANDATES 1920-48

British mandates

French mandates

(1932) Date of independence

0 Km   800
0 Miles   500

CHAPTER 1
THE
SOURCES
OF CONFLICT

The Middle East has for long been subject to both internal and external problems. Its position astride trade and communications routes and, more recently, its vast deposits of oil have ensured a high degree of interference by outside powers. Its volatile mix of ethnic and religious groupings, overlaid by the demands of nationalism, has made rivalry between the countries of the region a persistent problem. In such circumstances, violence is inevitable.

It is not easy to define "the Middle East." The term has its origins in the 19th century, when the world was centered on the colonial powers of Europe and outlying regions were described according to their direction and distance from the capitals of Britain, France or Germany. Thus "the East" was a general description of those countries, colonies and dependent territories which lay beyond the eastern borders of the Mediterranean, and was divided, quite logically, into "Near," "Middle" and "Far" according to distance.

Initially, the Near East included those areas under the rule of the Ottoman (Turkish) Empire. The Middle East denoted the independent countries of Persia (Iran) and Afghanistan which were useful as a buffer between the expanding empires of Russia and Britain.

The Far East described those regions even further afield, including China and Southeast Asia. With the collapse of the Ottoman Empire during the First World War (1914-18), the term Near East became irrelevant and the countries involved were included in a wider definition of Middle East. Even then, the outer limits of the region were, and still are, vague.

The area's extent

For the purposes of this book, the Middle East is taken to include the countries of Egypt, Israel, Jordan, Lebanon, Syria, Iraq, Iran, Saudi Arabia, North and South Yemen and the Gulf States (Kuwait, Bahrain, Qatar, the United Arab Emirates and Oman). Excluded are Turkey (regarded as part of Europe because of its membership of the North Atlantic Treaty Organization defense alliance), Libya, Sudan, Ethiopia and Somalia (all of which are undeniably African countries) and Afghanistan (part of what is now called "west Asia"), although they are included in some definitions.

Whatever the detail, however, it is essential to understand that the Middle East is not the same as the "Arab world." This usually includes Libya, Tunisia, Algeria and Morocco but not Iran and Israel. Nor is it the same as the "Muslim (Islamic) world," for much

the same reasons. In very general terms, the Middle East can be said to denote the landmass which connects the three great continents of Asia, Africa and Europe.

Its strategic position

This provides a clue to the importance of the region and to the principal reasons for its tradition as a center of conflict. The Middle East has always occupied a position of enormous strategic significance to outside powers. Being in the middle of intercontinental affairs, it has acted as a center of communications and trade. Spices and silks from China were brought by camel or by ship to the markets of Mesopotamia (Iraq) or the eastern Mediterranean, where they mingled with slaves and ivory from Africa and with manufactured goods from Europe.

The mixture of cultures created a vibrant society out of which new political and religious ideas emerged, but the enormous wealth engendered by the markets also ensured a high degree of outside interference as countries fought for exclusive control. In recent times, this situation has been made worse by the discovery and exploitation of oil, giving the Middle East (and especially the Gulf States) an added importance in the eyes of the industrialized world.

The Turkish commander of troops in Palestine during the First World War, 1914-18.

The Suez Canal

For centuries it was the Turks who enjoyed control of much of what we now call the Middle East, and it was not until the 19th century that this began to wane. The maritime powers of Europe (particularly the British and the French) had long recognized the value of trade with the region, but it was the construction of the Suez Canal in the 1860s – a project largely funded by the French – which persuaded them to establish a more permanent presence.

Once the Canal was opened, linking the Mediterranean to the Red Sea through Egyptian territory, it effectively halved the journey time between Europe and the Far East. The colonial powers soon saw that it was essential that the Canal did not fall into the hands of potential enemies. They might then threaten to close it in the event of a crisis or war.

The European powers intervene

This was particularly worrisome to the British, who depended heavily on trade with India, and their interest in the Middle East increased dramatically as soon as the Canal opened in 1869. Purchase of shares in the Suez Canal Company (the body which administered the waterway and took the profits from the tolls paid by canal users) gave Britain equality with the French. However, Britain also realized that she needed to have physical control of territories bordering the Canal or dominating its approaches.

As early as 1878, the island of Cyprus in the eastern Mediterranean (useful for monitoring the northern approaches to the Canal) passed into British hands; in 1882 Egypt was occupied, giving the British control of land on either side of the waterway; and in 1897 Britain occupied Sudan, extending that control further down the west bank of the Red Sea. Further south still, where the Red Sea flows into the Arabian Sea, the Bab el Mandeb Strait (a "choke-point" which could easily be blocked by an enemy) became equally important. Britain already had a coaling station at Aden, on the east bank of the strait, and by the end of the century had added part of Somaliland on the west.

By comparison, the French had done badly. Their shares in the Suez Canal Company were clearly valuable, and the territorial holdings of Djibouti and French Somaliland gave them a useful foothold at the southern end of the Red Sea, but they had failed to gain control of Egypt or Sudan. French influence among the pro-European Christians in the Turkish province of "Greater Syria" seemed poor compensation.

The First World War

In 1914, the First World War broke out. Britain and France fought on the same side against Germany, Austria-Hungary and Turkey and this led to a lessening of friction between the two colonial powers. Both intended to use the conflict to further their aims in the Middle East. Once again, however, it was the British who held the advantage, being able to divert part of their armed forces to campaigns in the region. By 1917, British and Empire troops were fighting the Turks in both Palestine (modern-day Israel) and Mesopotamia (modern-day Iraq). Britain also supported a revolt against Turkish rule in the Arabian peninsula, led by Hussein ibn Ali, the Sherif of Mecca. The British effort was coordinated by Colonel T. E. Lawrence ("Lawrence of Arabia").

These actions left them in a dominant position at the ensuing peace conference, where it became known that

Turkish troops man a machine-gun post, 1917.

a secret deal had been signed with the French in 1916 (the Sykes-Picot Agreement). This divided the main Middle East territories between the European powers, with Arabia gaining independence under rulers friendly to Britain.

The postwar settlement

In the event, the "carve-up" was supervised by the League of Nations, an international body set up after the First World War, and the territories transferred to Britain and France were not colonies but "mandates," held on behalf of the League on the strict understanding that they would be prepared for eventual independence. Even so, the physical presence of British troops, who had captured the key cities of Baghdad (Iraq), Jerusalem (Palestine) and Damascus (Syria) by the end of the war, ensured that Britain gained control of the most important areas in strategic terms.

In 1920, two separate mandates were granted to Britain – Palestine and the wide semi-desert tract east of the Jordan River (which became known as Trans-Jordan) on the one hand, and Mesopotamia on the other – while France had to make do with Greater Syria. Britain was now in a position to dominate the Middle East.

The fact that the French had to fight their way into Damascus in 1920 to establish a mandate of secondary importance, meant that they faced substantial problems and their presence was likely to be short-lived. To strengthen their position they set up a pro-European enclave known as Lebanon from among their Christian allies in the western part of Greater Syria. However, this was to produce more problems than it solved.

Religious splits

It would be wrong to imply from this that the British presence was trouble-free. They encountered problems which are still apparent today. High on the list was the question of religion, for the region contains a plethora of different beliefs, most of which are mutually hostile. The Middle East is the birthplace of the three main monotheistic (single god) religions of the world – Judaism, Christianity and Islam. It also contains important shrines, which people are willing to die for should they fall into the hands of a rival religious group.

As early as the 12th and 13th centuries, Christian knights from Europe fought the Crusades against the "infidels" of Islam. However, the rivalry between Judaism and Islam has caused the most lasting problems, particularly when overlaid by the territorial

and nationalist demands of Israel and her Arab neighbors in the modern world. Even within the Islamic faith, differences of doctrine have caused problems.

Founded by the prophet Mohammed in the 7th century AD, the Islamic religion split into two rival sects – the Shi'ites and the Sunnis – on his death, chiefly over the issue of who should succeed the prophet. The Shi'ites preferred his son-in-law, Ali, while the Sunnis backed the prophet's father-in-law, Abu Bakr. Today this split is characterized by extreme violence. Shi'ites form majorities in present-day Iran (where they control the government of the country), Iraq, North Yemen and Bahrain, with substantial minorities in Lebanon, Syria, Turkey, Pakistan and Afghanistan, but most Muslim countries tend to be governed by Sunni ruling classes.

Arab nationalism

Such splits already existed when the British assumed their new responsibilities in the Middle East in 1920, but were made much worse by the development of another pressure, that of Arab nationalism. Just as the French encountered local opposition from Arab peoples more interested in independence than a new form of imperial occupation, so the British came up against a mounting tide of nationalist feeling.

To a certain extent, this was their own fault. By supporting the Arab revolt under Hussein ibn Ali during the First World War, they had encouraged expectations of independence. In 1925, various territories in the Arabian peninsula came together to form an independent Saudi Arabia. This further raised Arab hopes for independence. Another complication was that the British tried to ensure their influence by manipulating local politics, supporting members of Hussein's family as rulers of Trans-Jordan, Iraq and Saudi Arabia. This caused resentment and was beset by family and tribal quarrels.

By 1928, Trans-Jordan had become virtually independent and by 1932 the mandate over Iraq had ceased. Nevertheless, Britain insisted on retaining a strong military presence, aware that internal conflict was simmering beneath the surface. The emergence of separate countries also denied the Arabs a common voice. By dividing the Arab people into more inward-looking national blocs, a powerful ethnic pressure was broken up. The divisions would continue to undermine the Arab cause, particularly as territorial rivalries between the new countries also emerged.

In the Arabian peninsula, for example, Saudi Arabia (the dominant country there) laid claim to the coastal enclaves of the Gulf States, while Iraq aimed to take over Kuwait; in the eastern Mediterranean, Syria refused (and continues to refuse) to accept the creation of Lebanon as a separate country, regarding it as part of Syrian territory.

The Jewish problem

If the Arabs had found a single leader, the second major problem encountered by the British – that of the Jews in Palestine – might not have been allowed to develop. Once again, the problem was of Britain's own making. In November 1917, at a time when Britain needed Jewish support both at home and in the United States for the war effort, Britain's Foreign Secretary, Arthur Balfour, made a written promise that his country would "view with favor" the creation of a "Jewish homeland" in Palestine once the fighting was over. The so-called Balfour Declaration was to become a key document in the modern history of the Middle East, creating an ethnic and religious divide which is still a major cause of conflict in the region.

Zionist demands

Pressure for a return of the Jews to the ancient "homelands" in what was now British-controlled Palestine came from a group of Jews known as Zionists. Led by a Hungarian Jew, Theodor Herzl, whose book *The Jewish State* was highly influential, the Zionists had begun their campaign for a return to the "Israel" of antiquity in the 1890s. Without the pressures of the First World War, it is unlikely that much would have come of the scheme. As it was, Britain could see long-term advantages in the creation of a European-style presence in Palestine. It would help to protect the eastward approaches to the Suez Canal.

It soon became apparent, however, that their definition of a homeland for the Jews was quite different from that of the Zionist leadership. To the British, the idea was to create a Jewish presence, which would coexist with the indigenous Arabs of Palestine. The British probably never envisaged the Jews as constituting more than 30 per cent of the total population. Unfortunately, the Zionists had other ideas.

In the 1920s and 1930s Jewish immigration increased dramatically and the new settlers started buying land from absentee Arab owners. They wanted to set up self-contained, virtually independent *kibbutzim* (settlements). It soon became clear that the

A British soldier body-searches an Arab in Jerusalem, 1938.

Zionists were only interested in the establishment of an independent Jewish state. As early as 1929, when the Jewish National Fund purchased land from which some 2,500 Arab farmers were then evicted, riots and disturbances broke out, principally in Jerusalem and Hebron. The British restored order, but were forced to face the fact that Palestine was unlikely to remain quiet.

The Arab revolt in Palestine

The situation grew worse when Adolf Hitler came to power in Germany in 1933 and began to persecute the Jewish minority there. This provoked much sympathy for the Zionist cause. In 1936, as levels of Jewish immigration rose and Arab resentment reached new heights, the British tried to lay down immigration quotas, but this merely sparked off an Arab revolt. It was to last for three years, until the outbreak of the Second World War in 1939, and necessitated the commitment of large numbers of British forces.

In 1937, a special government commission recommended splitting Palestine into Jewish and Arab areas, with Jerusalem and the port of Haifa remaining under mandate control, but this pleased no one. Finally, in 1939, Britain promised complete independence for

Palestine as a whole, with Jews and Arabs enjoying equal rights and restrictions imposed on the number of Jews allowed to enter the country. The Second World War, however, halted any further progress.

Egyptian independence

Meanwhile, the British had also been experiencing problems in Egypt, where demands for independence (Britain had declared the country to be a "protectorate" in 1914) increased as soon as the First World War was over. These were satisfied in 1922, but Britain retained the right to guard the Suez Canal, to defend the country against outside aggression, to safeguard foreign interests in the area and to continue to administer Sudan. The latter territory was traditionally part of Egypt, so the British conditions, together with the maintenance of a large garrison around the Canal, were guaranteed to annoy Egyptian nationalists.

The unrest continued until, in 1936, the young King Farouk signed a fresh treaty with the British. This gave Egypt freedom to conduct her own foreign policy, although it did not lead to a British withdrawal from either Sudan or the Canal Zone. As Farouk's agreement to these conditions led to internal opposition to his rule, particularly among nationalist army officers, it was likely that more trouble was about to develop.

With the outbreak of the Second World War in 1939, Egypt broke off relations with Germany, but did not declare war. However, a large number of British

Egyptian women protest against British martial law, 1922.

troops were sent to Egypt and a major campaign was fought against the Italians (from Libya, an Italian possession) and Germany between 1940 and 1942, in which the prize was control of the Suez Canal. Both in 1941 and 1942, when it looked as if the Germans might be victorious in North Africa, there was a wave of pro-German feeling among the Egyptian nationalists, but this was contained by the British.

Jewish women working the land in Palestine, in the 1930s.

Problems for the British

Elsewhere in the Middle East, there were other problems for the British to face. In April 1941, there was a pro-German *coup d'etat* (takeover of government) in Iraq, and the vital British airbase at Habbaniyah was besieged by elements of the Iraqi Army. The British sent in forces to crush this and effectively occupied the country. They did the same with Syria and Lebanon, where German influence seemed to be on the increase.

The problem here had arisen in June 1940, when France had been defeated by Germany. The French administration of the mandated territories had been transferred to the pro-German government at Vichy. By early 1941, the British were alarmed that the area could come under complete German control. This would pose a threat to Palestine and the eastern approaches to the Canal, so they decided to invade, occupying Lebanon and Syria for the rest of the war.

The invasion of Iran

The third area to cause problems was Iran, for although a long-established independent country, its strategic importance as a source of oil (essential in the new age of mechanized warfare) and as a route for the delivery of supplies to the Soviet Union, could not be ignored. In 1939, Iran declared neutrality, but as with Iraq, Lebanon and Syria, it soon became obvious that the Germans intended to extend their influence there. In August 1941, both the Soviet Union and Britain demanded that the Iranians expel all German nationals and, when this did not happen, they both invaded the country, dividing its administration between them for as long as the war continued.

The involvement of British troops in the occupation of Iran, Iraq, Lebanon and Syria was clearly understandable in strategic terms, as it ensured the security of key areas in a world war. It also signified the declining influence of the other powers, particularly the French. When the war ended in 1945, the French had little choice but to grant independence to their former mandates.

In 1945, the British withdrew from both Iraq and Iran (despite, in the latter case, a marked reluctance by the Soviets to do the same), but it was apparent that Britain now occupied the key positions in the Middle East. With continued presence in Egypt, Sudan, Palestine, Cyprus, Somaliland and Aden, as well as significant influence in Trans-Jordan, Iraq and the smaller Gulf States, her position seemed unassailable. It was not to last.

Palestinian problems

Britain's influence began to wane most dramatically in Palestine, where the deep ethnic and religious divides of the 1930s persisted throughout the Second World War. During that conflict, the very existence of Palestine was called into doubt once General Erwin Rommel's *Afrika Korps* had advanced deep into Egypt in 1942. Both Jews and Arabs joined the British in their war effort, but this did not affect their long-term demands for independence or the creation of separate homelands.

Some Jewish hardliners, for example, continued to regard Britain as a greater enemy than the Germans and were prepared to mount attacks on the "occupying forces" while the war was going on. The most extreme organization which emerged was the *Lohamei Heruth Israel* (Fighters for the Freedom of Israel) or LEHI, led by Avraham Stern, a Polish Jew who had come to Palestine in 1940. His group was known to the British as the Stern Gang and committed many atrocities. Stern was killed in 1942, but his group lived on and, two years later, gave notice of their future intentions by assassinating the British Minister Resident in Cairo, Lord Moyne.

Slightly less extreme, but of greater long-term significance, was the *Irgun Zvai Leumi* (National Military Organization) under Menachem Begin, a future prime minister of Israel. The *Irgun* announced a revolt against continued British rule in 1944, although it refrained from carrying out attacks on British military targets while the war against Hitler was still continuing. Instead it attacked police stations, tax offices and other symbols of British rule. All this implied that, once the war was over, Britain was going to face substantial opposition.

Thus, by 1945, many of the causes of conflict in the Middle East were already apparent. The deep religious divides between Jews and Muslims, and Shi'ite and Sunni Islamic sects, were a major force. They were coupled with new demands for independence or nationalist satisfaction, often manifested in territorial disputes. On top of all this, the area was too important in strategic and economic terms to be left alone.

By 1945 British influence was under pressure, especially in Palestine but with the growing importance of oil to many industrialized countries, outside interference in the affairs of the Middle East was likely to persist. If the region is likened to a cauldron of unrest, all the ingredients for continued trouble were present in abundance.

The last British troops leave Israel, 1948.

CHAPTER 2
ARAB VERSUS JEW

Of all the rivalries of the Middle East since 1945, that between Israel and its Arab neighbors has been the most persistent, producing an endless succession of crises and wars. As soon as Israel emerged as a separate country in 1948, Arab armies attacked, and it was only through superior fighting skills that Israel survived at all. The refinement of those skills led to Israeli victories in 1956 and 1967, but did nothing to solve the basic problem of the Palestinians.

With the end of the war in 1945, Syria, Lebanon and Trans-Jordan were granted full independence. Together with Egypt, Saudi Arabia and Iran, they became founder members of the United Nations (UN). This was the organization set up on October 24, 1945, which would according to its charter ". . . save succeeding generations from the scourge of war . . . reaffirm faith in fundamental human rights and promote social progress." Both Syria and Lebanon immediately used their membership to complain, in February 1946, that the British and French were not withdrawing their troops fast enough. These withdrawals were completed by the end of that summer.

Iran had a similar problem. While the British had withdrawn their forces from the country at the end of the war, the Soviets had not done so. In January 1946, Iran took the matter to the United Nations. She stated that the Russians had prevented her from sending in troops to one of her border provinces to put down a separatist movement, which she accused the Soviet Union of supporting. In May 1946, the Soviets withdrew. Quickly, the British and the Americans moved in, not with troops, but with money in order to secure further oil concessions.

The Palestinian problem

Palestine, however, remained the focus of the Middle East's immediate postwar problems. Until a solution to the Jewish-Arab struggle could be found, Britain had no intention of giving up her mandate. Indeed, she made Palestine her Middle East base, sending additional troops there.

Matters quickly came to a head with the problem of the European Jews who had survived Hitler's persecution. Many, after enduring the concentration camps, wanted to leave Europe for good and start life anew in Palestine. To allow them unrestricted settlement in Palestine would have made the existing conflict worse.

A Jewish home

The Palestinian Jews, who had now set up the Jewish Agency, were determined that, since the war had been fought and won, the Jewish National Homeland should become a fact as soon as possible. The underground armies of the *Irgun* and the LEHI now joined the moderate "home guard," the *Haganah*, which had been formed to protect Jewish settlements during the prewar period. Together they launched a wave of attacks on communications and the police at the end of October 1945.

Within two weeks, the British announced that they were revoking their 1939 plan for separate Jewish and Arab states and that they were restricting Jewish immigration to 1,500 people per month. This pleased neither side and unrest increased. The British Army was called in to help the police, who could not cope.

The situation quickly worsened and more British troops had to be brought in. The violence would not die down. Britain now turned to the United States for help in dealing with the problem. In April 1946, a joint committee recommended that 100,000 Jewish refugees be allowed in from Europe, but only if both Arabs and Jews surrendered their arms. This again failed to stop the violence; in fact Jewish terrorists stepped up attacks on the British. This culminated in the blowing up of the King David Hotel in Jerusalem, which the British were using for offices, by the *Irgun* on July 22, 1946. Some 91 people were killed and 45 injured.

The United Nations Special Committee

By the beginning of 1947, realizing that they were in an impossible situation, the British had had enough. In April, they referred the matter to the United Nations. A committee was set up (the United Nations Special Committee on Palestine – UNSCOP), with members

The King David Hotel following the bomb attack, 1946.

from 11 member countries, to investigate the problem.

There was some opposition from the Arab League, which had been formed by Egypt, Syria, Lebanon, Iraq, Jordan, Saudi Arabia and Yemen in 1945. Their objection was that the committee was not looking into Palestinian independence and that it would ignore the interests of the inhabitants of Palestine. Indeed, they feared that the Palestinian problem was going to be too closely bound up with the plight of the Jewish refugees from Europe. This fear seemed to have some foundation when the committee began its investigations in June 1947.

From 1940 onwards, the British had had to cope with ships filled with illegal Jewish immigrants crossing the Mediterranean and trying to land them in Palestine.

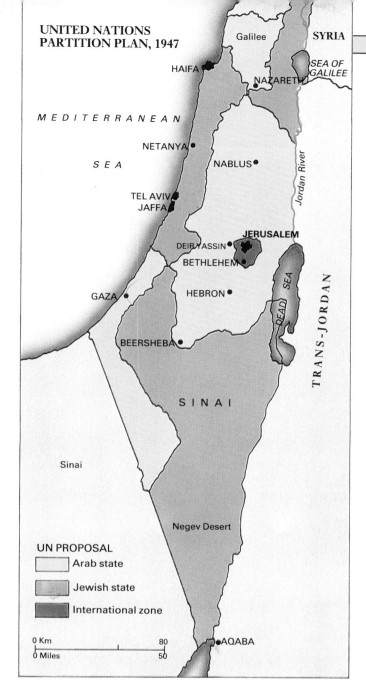

**UNITED NATIONS
PARTITION PLAN, 1947**

MEDITERRANEAN
SEA

Galilee
SYRIA
SEA OF
GALILEE
HAIFA
NAZARETH

NETANYA
NABLUS

TEL AVIV
JAFFA

JERUSALEM
DEIR YASSIN
BETHLEHEM

GAZA
HEBRON

DEAD SEA

TRANS-JORDAN
Jordan River

BEERSHEBA

SINAI

Sinai

Negev Desert

UN PROPOSAL
Arab state
Jewish state
International zone

0 Km   80
0 Miles   50

AQABA

refused to talk to the committee. At the end of August, it submitted its report to the United Nations.

The majority report recommended dividing Palestine into two independent states, one Jewish and the other Arab, and giving Jerusalem international status under the administration of the United Nations. A minority report recommended a federal state, consisting of an Arab and Jewish state, with Jerusalem as the federal capital. The United Nations now summoned all three parties, British, Arabs and Jews.

The British said that they would not use force to impose a policy. If no settlement were achieved, they would withdraw their troops and administration regardless. The Arabs resented any partition of the country and did not see why the Jews, who were still the minority in Palestine, should be given their land. Only the Jews favored the United Nations' proposal, but only on the condition that the Jewish state be established immediately, with complete control over immigration.

The British pull out

Nonetheless, the majority proposal was adopted by the United Nations General Assembly at the end of November 1947. The British mandate would end on May 15 and all British troops would withdraw by August 1, 1948. The violence between Jew and Arab intensified. On Christmas Day 1947 alone, more than 100 Jews and Arabs were killed, and the *Irgun* massacred 254 Arab men, women and children at the village of Deir Yassin as a reprisal.

The British Army found itself in the middle, being shot at by both sides. By spring 1948, it had largely given up trying to control the situation and was concentrated in enclaves around Jerusalem, Jaffa and Haifa. Jewish forces were fighting to establish their hold over the territory allocated to them by the United Nations. With the expiration of the mandate, the Jews immediately proclaimed the state of Israel and the Arab League responded by sending 30,000 troops into Palestine.

The United Nations had already sent a team to Palestine to try and set up a truce between Jew and Arab, and a mediator, Count Folke Bernadotte, President of the Swedish Red Cross, was now appointed. On June 11, a four-week truce was arranged. Meanwhile, the British troops began their evacuation, some going overland to Egypt, while the others went by ship from the port of Haifa. By June 30, 1948 the evacuation was complete.

In July 1947, one such ship, the *Exodus*, carrying 4,000 European Jews, was intercepted by the Royal Navy and ordered to go back to the south of France, from where it had sailed. The Jews refused to disembark there and so the *Exodus* was sent round to the north German port of Hamburg and the refugees forcibly removed. The story was reported in newspaper headlines around the world as an example of the inhuman British treatment of the Jews, and became part of Jewish folklore.

The committee's report

Meanwhile, the violence in Palestine continued. The UN committee visited Palestine, Lebanon, Syria and Trans-Jordan, as well as displaced persons' camps in Germany and Austria. The Palestinian Arabs, however,

The truces

The United Nations-imposed truce saved the infant Israeli state. Attacked on four fronts by five Arab armies – Egyptian, Jordanian, Syrian, Lebanese and Iraqi – the makeshift Israeli forces were hard-pressed. The ceasefire enabled them to obtain further arms from sympathizers in Europe and the United States. It broke down on July 7 when the Arab League armies renewed their offensive. Israel survived by pursuing a policy of aggressive defense, mounting limited counterattacks on each front in turn in order to keep the Arabs off balance. Ten days later, the United Nations truce team managed to arrange a further ceasefire.

The second truce lasted longer than the first and Count Bernadotte used it as an opportunity to try to find a lasting territorial solution to the problem. Since the Israeli forces in the Negev desert in the south of Palestine were totally cut off, he proposed that this should be given to the Arabs while the Jews received western Galilee in return.

The Israeli leadership under David Ben-Gurion felt itself forced to accept this, but not the more extremist *Irgun* and LEHI, who still retained some independence outside the newly formed Israeli Defense Force. It was probably they who shot Bernadotte and the chief French UN observer in Jerusalem on September 19. Realizing that these murders would condemn Israel in the eyes of the world, Ben-Gurion ordered the *Irgun* to hand over its arms to the Israeli Defense Force and arrested 200 LEHI members.

Renewed fighting

The truce lasted until October, giving the Israelis the opportunity to obtain further arms from abroad. It was broken when they attacked the Egyptians in the Negev on the pretext that they had not allowed food convoys through their lines. In six days, the Israelis linked up with their beleaguered forces and cleared the coastal strip. They now turned to the north. By the end of October, they had virtually cleared Galilee of Arabs and even occupied a strip of Lebanon, knocking that country out of the war.

In spite of numerous calls by the United Nations for a ceasefire, the fighting went on. From now on, it was concentrated in the south of Palestine. The Israelis believed that the United Nations still favored the Bernadotte plan and that they would be forced to surrender the Negev. In order to prevent this, they launched a series of attacks on the Egyptians designed to drive them out of Palestine and bring them to the negotiating table. These were so successful that the Israelis even entered Egyptian territory in Sinai, cutting off an Egyptian army in the Gaza area. The United Nations considered that the Israelis had gone too far and they were forced to withdraw from their gains in Egypt, but not before there were clashes between Israeli and British aircraft.

Armistice

The Israeli victories were sufficient for the Egyptians to be prepared to begin peace talks. These were arranged by Bernadotte's successor, Ralph J. Bunche. On February 24, 1949, Egypt and Israel signed an armistice agreement on the island of Rhodes. This allowed Israel to retain the Negev, but the Egyptians

THE NEW FRONTIERS:
THE ARAB-ISRAELI WAR, 1948-49

Israeli territory, May 1948
Israeli gains by November 1948
Israeli gains by January 1949
Israeli borders by June 1949

0 Km 80
0 Miles 50

ARAB INVASION PLANS, MAY 1948
INVASION FORCES
Lebanese
Syrian
Palestinian
Iraqi
Arab Legion (Jordanian)
Egyptian

0 Km 80
0 Miles 50

were given the coastal area around Gaza, which became known as the Gaza Strip.

Other armistice agreements followed. One with Lebanon was signed in March, with the Israelis withdrawing their forces from that country, and those with Jordan and Syria were signed in April and July respectively. In all cases it was accepted that the United Nations should supervise the implementation of the agreements.

The new state of Israel

The 1948-49 Arab-Israeli war left three-quarters of what had been Palestine incorporated in the state of Israel. There was no question now of a Palestinian Arab state being formed. About 725,000 Palestinians left their homes and became refugees. Some 160,000 Palestinian Arabs remained and found themselves under Jewish rule. The remainder either came under Egyptian rule in the Gaza Strip or that of Jordan in the Nablus-Hebron area west of the Jordan River. This became known as the West Bank.

Jerusalem, in spite of the United Nations' efforts to make it a demilitarized city under international control, was divided between Israel and Jordan. None of the Arab states was prepared to recognize the state of Israel and she in turn remained deeply suspicious of them. The Palestinian Arabs, especially those remaining in Israel, harbored an ever deepening resentment at being deprived of their homeland. The war had solved nothing.

Coups in Arab states

Throughout the next few years there were constant border clashes, except on the border with Lebanon. These were primarily raids by Palestinian Arabs into Israel, to which the latter replied in kind.

Within the countries of the Arab League there was deep bitterness over the military defeats which they had suffered. This resulted in a number of coups. In Syria, the government was overthrown by an army general shortly after the armistice with Israel had been signed. Two years later, in 1951, the general was himself overthrown and further military coups occurred during the next few years.

In July 1951, King Abdullah of Jordan, who had been secretly working towards a permanent peace with Israel, was killed in Jerusalem by agents of the Mufti, the Muslim religious leader living in the city. A year later, Abdullah's grandson, the youthful Hussein, who had been educated in Britain, succeeded to the throne.

Egyptian nationalist grievances

In Egypt, grievances among the nationalists had been growing. King Farouk had gained an international reputation as a playboy, which the nationalists felt was not appropriate for the nation's leader. The continued British military presence in the Canal Zone, bordering the Suez Canal, was resented. A series of weak Egyptian governments had done little to improve conditions in the country. Finally, there was bitterness over Egypt's defeat in the recent war against Israel.

Much of the nationalist hatred was directed towards the British. The nationalists also attacked Egyptian institutions, even killing the prime minister at the end of 1948. At the beginning of 1950, a new government was formed by the *Wafd* Party, which had been founded at the end of 1918 to pursue total Egyptian independence through peaceful means. During 1950 and 1951 it negotiated with the British in an attempt to regain the Canal Zone and Egyptian hold over Sudan.

The British, however, stuck rigidly to the 1936 treaty, and all the Egyptians could do in the end was to declare that they had torn it up. The *Wafd* government was still not prepared to use force against the British, who ruthlessly dealt with terrorist acts committed by nationalists in the Canal Zone.

Palestinian refugees leave Israel, 1948.

Military coup

Discontent with both the king and government rose alarmingly. Towards the end of 1949 a group of Egyptian officers had formed a group called the Free Officers' Committee. Among them were Gamal Abdel Nasser and Anwar el-Sadat. Throughout the next three years they discreetly enlisted many other officers to their cause. On July 23, 1952, the Free Officers acted. The government was deposed and a military *junta* (council), with General Mohammed Naguib as its figurehead, was installed instead.

King Farouk was forced to abdicate and went in permanent exile to Monaco. His son, the infant Crown Prince, was proclaimed in his place. Within a year, however, he had been removed and a republic had been set up. Political parties were banned and the country ruled through the Revolution Command Council.

The Revolution Command Council reopened negotiations with the British. In February 1953 agreement was reached whereby Sudan would be granted independence within three years and this became a fact in 1956. Talks were also held on the Canal Zone. Eventually, in October 1954, the British agreed to vacate it, although they would be allowed to use it as a military base in time of war. Both countries also recognized the Suez Canal as an international waterway.

Iran

It was not just the members of the Arab League who had to endure internal upheaval during the early 1950s. In Iran a nationalist movement had risen in the late 1940s. It resented the fact that its oil resources had been virtually taken over by the British and Americans.

In 1951, Dr Mohammed Mossadeq's National Front seized power and nationalized (confiscated on behalf of his country) all oil assets held by foreigners. The Shah was forced to flee the country. The British imposed an economic blockade which caused severe difficulties for the country. The Soviet Union supported Mossadeq and, fearful that the West would be denied this vital source of oil, the United States engineered a coup in 1953 which enabled the Shah to depose Mossadeq and regain his throne.

The Baghdad Pact

By 1954, the real power in Egypt was in Nasser's hands and in April of that year he became prime minister. He was determined to unite the Arab states in a "holy" war against Israel. In spite of United Nations' efforts to maintain a truce along Israel's borders, the raids continued.

One blow to Nasser's plan, however, was the formation of the Baghdad Pact in 1955. This was an attempt by Britain to maintain her influence in the Middle East and was a defense agreement signed by Britain, Turkey, Iraq and Pakistan. She had also tried to get Jordan to join, but pro-Nasser elements managed to influence the Jordanian government, which adopted an anti-Western stance. In order to keep his hold on power, King Hussein was forced, in 1954, to expel the British officers serving in his Arab Legion.

General Mohammed Naguib surrounded by his staff (Gamal Abdel Nasser is on his right) shortly after the coup, July 1952.

Nasser aligns with the Soviet Union

Nasser saw the formation of the Baghdad Pact as an attempt to isolate Egypt. He therefore began to turn increasingly to the Soviet Union and Eastern bloc. In April 1955, he attended the Bandung Conference of Afro-Asian states and openly declared his opposition to "imperialism" - the taking over of countries by other countries intent on creating their empires – and military alliances. From then on, he became increasingly anti-Western.

In September 1955 he arranged to purchase arms from Czechoslovakia, declaring that this was because Britain and the United States had refused to supply him with any, and that the United States was arming Israel. In May 1956 he recognized Communist China. To Britain and the United States, it seemed that Egypt was now joining the Communist bloc.

They registered their protest over Nasser's plans to construct a showpiece dam at Aswan on the Nile. Having originally offered money for it, they suddenly, in July 1956, withdrew from the project. The Soviets, too, had made a similar offer and this was now accepted, marking the beginning of an era of Soviet influence over Egypt.

The Suez Canal Crisis

By this time, Nasser had become President of Egypt, having deposed Naguib the previous November. He responded to the US and British withdrawal from the Aswan Dam project by declaring, on July 26, 1956, that he was nationlizing the Suez Canal Company.

Britain, the United States and France, who had always been a major shareholder in the Canal Company, retaliated by freezing all Egypt's money and holdings in their countries. Britain was convinced that the Egyptians did not have the technical expertise to run the Canal and saw a threat to her Middle East oil supplies and communications with the Far East. Both she and France were determined to use force to regain control of the Canal.

The United States, on the other hand, was against this. Force smacked of imperialism, which she strongly opposed. Instead, she proposed an international organization to run the Canal, but Nasser rejected this because he wanted to show that he could run the Canal just as efficiently as the British and French. The matter now went before the United Nations. In the meantime, convinced that military action was the only answer, Britain and France secretly began to organize forces to regain the Canal.

Israel intervenes

The 1955 Egyptian-Czechoslovakian arms deal and the formation of a joint Egyptian-Syrian military command in October of that year convinced Israel that Egypt was about to attack her. This belief was strengthened when Jordan joined the joint military command in 1956. Furthermore, Egypt was preventing Israeli ships from using the Suez Canal and the waters around her territory. A compensating factor, however, was that Israel enjoyed closer relations with France, who was becoming increasingly irritated with Nasser's support for the independence movement against French rule in Algeria. France began to supply Israel with arms.

In September 1956, the French informed Israel of the joint plan with the British to regain the Suez Canal and invited her to take part. By this time, Israel had made up her mind that the only way she could reduce the mounting pressure, created by Arab rearmament and the cross-border raids, was to launch a pre-emptive attack. She was, therefore, willing to co-operate with the British and French. The two super-powers, the United States and the Soviet Union, were otherwise preoccupied. The United States was in the middle of a presidential election and the Soviet Union was grappling with demands for greater freedom in Poland and Hungary.

The attack on Sinai

It was the Israelis who struck first. Their aims were to knock out the Egyptian forces in Sinai so that they no longer posed a threat, to destroy the Palestinian terrorist organization and seize the Straits of Tiran so that the Israeli port of Elat at the head of the Gulf of Aqaba could be opened once more to shipping. They launched their attack on the Egyptians in Sinai on October 29, 1956, catching them by surprise.

Israeli paratroops quickly seized the key Mitla Pass and ground troops from Kuntilla linked up with them. To the north, in central Sinai, tanks advanced to outflank Egyptian forces around Abu Aweigila and break through the Egyptian defenses. Next day, October 30, the British warned the United Nations that, unless the fighting ended quickly, passage through the Suez Canal would be endangered. They and the French had warned Egypt and Israel that, unless they withdrew to 16 km (10 miles) from the Canal within 12 hours, they would have no option but to intervene. Both the United States and Soviet Union put up draft resolutions ordering Israel to withdraw behind the 1949 armistice line, but these were blocked by Britain and France.

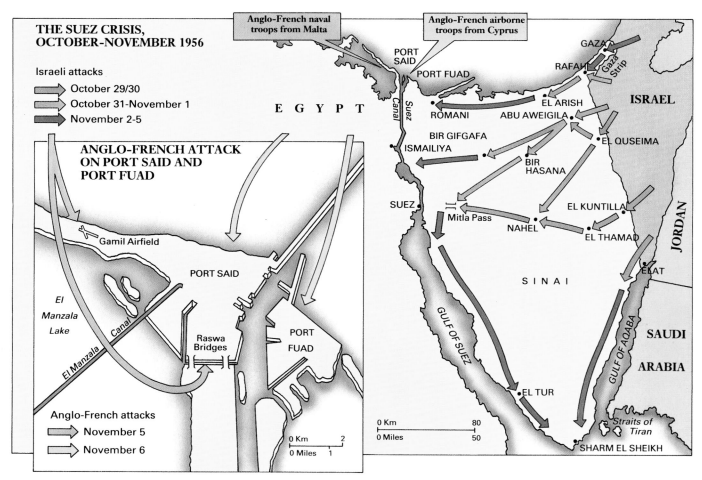

THE SUEZ CRISIS, OCTOBER-NOVEMBER 1956

Israeli attacks
- October 29/30
- October 31-November 1
- November 2-5

ANGLO-FRENCH ATTACK ON PORT SAID AND PORT FUAD

Anglo-French attacks
- November 5
- November 6

Britain and France join Israel

When Egypt announced that she had rejected the ultimatum, the French and British prepared for action and aircraft bombed air bases in Egypt on the 31st. On the next day, French and British amphibious task forces set sail from Malta and Algeria. In Britain, at least, there was much opposition to the use of force to solve the problem and this made the British government hesitate and lose purpose.

In the meantime, the Israeli offensive increased in momentum. Slicing through the Gaza Strip and central Sinai, the Israelis took large numbers of bewildered Egyptians prisoner and captured vast amounts of arms and equipment. Soon they had closed up to the Suez Canal. They now turned south and, by November 5, had reached Sharm el Sheikh at the entrance to the Gulf of Aqaba and had crossed over to the island of Tiran to destroy the Egyptian defenses there. Sinai was in Israeli hands.

On that same day, November 5, 1956, the Anglo-French landings finally took place. British and French paratroops dropped on Gamil airfield outside Port Said and vital bridges on the Port Said-Suez road respectively. Next day, British troops landed by sea at Port Said and French troops on the opposite bank of the Canal at Port Fuad. Egyptian resistance was light but they refused to surrender.

Ceasefire

The United Nations General Assembly, which had been in constant session, demanded an immediate ceasefire. The British now accepted that the United States would not support them. Their reputation in the world was now low – this was demonstrated by the rapid drop in the pound's value. Therefore, on the evening of the 6th, they accepted the ceasefire demand and the French were forced to follow suit. The Israelis, who had achieved all their aims in Sinai, had no objection and neither did Egypt, since she had gained worldwide sympathy.

The terms of the ceasefire were that a United Nations Emergency Force (UNEF), made up of member nations not involved in the conflict, would be sent to the area as soon as possible. British, French and Israeli forces were to withdraw from Egyptian territory and Egypt guaranteed rights of passage to all shipping through the Suez Canal and to Israeli ships in the Gulf of Aqaba.

British and French withdrawal was completed just before Christmas 1956 and that of the Israelis in March 1957. UNEF troops were stationed at Sharm el Sheikh and in the Gaza Strip. United Nations members also undertook to clear the Suez Canal.

It was Britain who suffered most from the Suez affair. The fact that it had taken her four months to gather together sufficient forces to take back the Canal showed that she could no longer be regarded as a first-class world power.

Nasser's reputation had been boosted, and he was now regarded as the champion of the Arab world. At the same time, Nasser had been driven further into the arms of the Soviet Union. Indeed, from now on it was the United States and the Soviet Union who would be rivals for influence over the Middle East.

Right: *French troops prepare for action, Port Said, 1956.*
Below: *British tank in the streets of Port Said, 1956.*

An uneasy peace

For the next few years, thanks to the UNEF presence, relative peace was maintained between Israel and Egypt in Sinai. This did not mean that Nasser recognized Israeli's right to exist. He realized that a much stronger alliance of Arab nations was needed to overthrow her. As a first step, Egypt and Syria were joined together as the United Arab Republic (UAR) in 1958. That same year the pro-West King Faisal of Iraq and many members of his family were murdered and a left-leaning military regime was set up.

Nasser also stirred up unrest in Lebanon and Jordan. In the former, civil war broke out and President Camille Chamoun turned to the Americans to support his government. A force of US Marines was landed from the Sixth Fleet, which was in the Mediterranean, in July 1958. The Marines remained there for 100 days and saw a stronger, but still moderate government under General Fuad Chehab installed. He enjoyed support from both Muslims and Christians. In Jordan the situation was much the same, and King Hussein called on Britain to help him. A brigade of paratroops was flown into Jordan in July 1958. It withdrew at the same time as the US Marines from Lebanon.

The Central Treaty Organization

Both Jordan and Lebanon had used the Baghdad Pact to appeal for British and US help and one of Nasser's aims was to see this destroyed and no longer a threat. His first success came when Iraq broke with it in March 1959. The Pact was then renamed the Central Treaty Organization (CENTO). In the meantime, Nasser continued his efforts to foster instability in Jordan, and in 1960 his agents murdered the Jordanian prime minister. There were also several unsuccessful attempts on the life of King Hussein.

In 1961 there was a major blow to Nasser's hopes. The Syrians withdrew from the United Arab Republic, on the grounds that Egypt was interfering too much in their affairs, and their nation became fully independent once more. That same year produced a crisis in another quarter. Oil-rich Kuwait was threatened with invasion from her envious northern neighbor Iraq, which tried to claim some of her territory. Kuwait appealed to the United Nations and asked Britain and Saudi Arabia for help. In July, British troops were sent there. They stayed until October, when the Arab League, of which Kuwait was a member, took over the task of defending her. The invasion threat came to nothing.

British problems in Yemen

Nasser's anti-imperialism and desire for Arab unity also began to make itself felt in the Arabian peninsula. The British still held the port of Aden, which they had acquired in 1839 as a coaling station for their ships sailing to and from India. There were also a number of surrounding tribal territories which they had formed into two "protectorates." The tribesmen in these were often unruly, and Nasser saw the chance to undermine the British position.

There was also independent Yemen, ruled by the Imam, to the north, which had always been suspicious of Britain, even though many Yemenis worked in Aden port. Faced with this growing Egyptian inspired threat, in 1959 the British joined the two protectorates into the Federation of South Arabia. Both Nasser and the Imam opposed this.

In 1961, however, the Imam died, his son was overthrown and a pro-Nasser republic was declared under General Abdullah Sallal. Many Yemenis objected and civil war broke out. Sallal made his determination to work toward the break up of the Federation of South Arabia very clear and Nasser sent troops to help him in his battle with the royalist tribesmen under the Imam's son, Badr. Nasser was to find himself committed here for the next six years. More serious was the fact that the kingdom of Saudi Arabia actively supported the royalists with arms.

In the meantime, Sallal and Nasser organized rebel nationalist groups to operate against the Federation. These based themselves in the mountainous Radfan, 96 km (60 miles) north of Aden. In January 1964 the British sent troops and by mid-summer had driven the rebels out. This only proved a temporary lull. While the British Government declared in July 1964 that South Arabia would be given independence by 1968, it still intended to maintain a military presence. The rebel groups were determined to gain power. To do this they used terrorist methods against the British in Aden. This lasted from the end of 1964 until the end of November 1967, when the British finally left. Aden, now called South Yemen, was in the hands of the victorious rebel group, the National Liberation Front.

The birth of the Palestine Liberation Organization

The United Nations peace-keepers had succeeded in keeping violence in Sinai at a low level. On the Syrian and, later, the Jordanian frontiers with Israel, where United Nations troops were not present, there were growing cross-border incidents.

In 1964 an Arab summit conference was held in Cairo. It decided that a Palestinian movement, the Palestine Liberation Organization (PLO), should be set up and given active support. The Arabs also resolved to divert the waters of the Jordan River, which would deprive Israel of two-thirds of her water. Both Lebanon and Syria began to put this into effect. Israel viewed this in the same way as she did the closing of the Straits of Tiran – as an act of war – and obstructed the work with artillery fire and air strikes.

The PLO was, from the start, determined to bring the Arab states into another war with Israel. It was the only way in which it could regain its homeland.

Thus, its terrorist acts became more provocative. The Ba'ath Party which ruled Syria had been cool towards Egypt ever since the break up of the United Arab Republic. They wanted to form a revolutionary alliance which excluded "reactionary states" like Saudi Arabia and Jordan. This was heightened in February 1966 when extremist army officers seized control.

At the same time, Nasser was falling out with Saudi Arabia over attempts to end the fighting in the Yemen. Because of this, Egypt and Syria came together again and signed an alliance in November 1966. Conscious of what might happen to him if he did not follow suit, King Hussein joined the alliance in May 1967.

British troops question an Arab involved in anti-British demonstrations in Aden, March 1967.

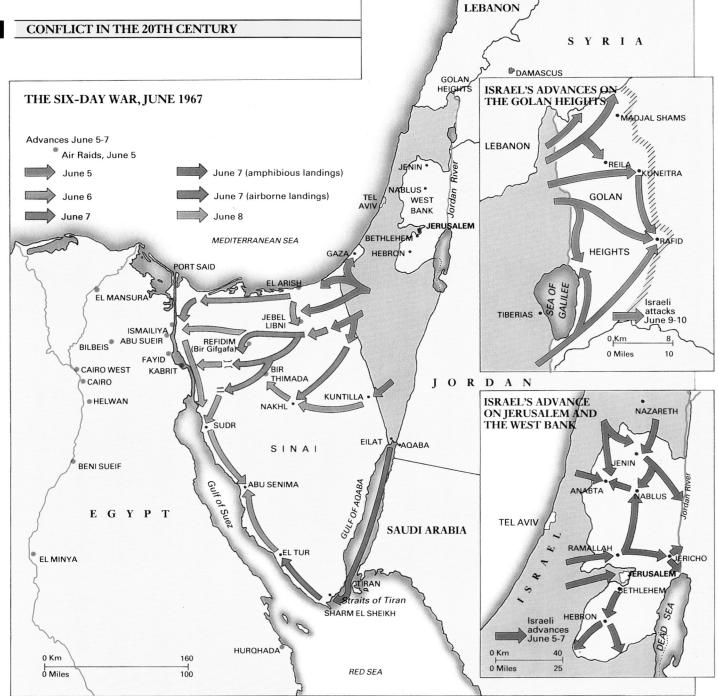

THE SIX-DAY WAR, JUNE 1967

Advances June 5-7
- Air Raids, June 5
- ➡ June 5
- ➡ June 6
- ➡ June 7
- ➡ June 7 (amphibious landings)
- ➡ June 7 (airborne landings)
- ➡ June 8

ISRAEL'S ADVANCES ON THE GOLAN HEIGHTS

Israeli attacks June 9-10

0 Km 8
0 Miles 10

ISRAEL'S ADVANCE ON JERUSALEM AND THE WEST BANK

Israeli advances June 5-7

0 Km 40
0 Miles 25

0 Km 160
0 Miles 100

Border clashes

Clashes between the Israeli and Syrian forces had been increasing. In early May 1967 the Soviet Union, playing on the Syrian fears that Israel might attack her, told Egypt that Israel was massing her army on the Syrian border. This was not true, but it was enough to make Nasser take steps to help his ally. He also saw the chance to restore his popularity, which had waned in the Arab world. Nasser could not take military action while UNEF was still in Sinai and on May 16 demanded its removal. At the same time he began to mobilize his forces. Within a week there were nearly 100,000 troops in the Sinai, backed up by 1,000 tanks,

in striking distance of the Israeli borders.

The United Nations Secretary-General U Thant asked Israel if she would accept UN forces on her side of the border in Sinai, but this was rejected. There was thus no option but to withdraw UNEF, although it would take some weeks to accomplish. There were mass demonstrations for war in Cairo and offers of support from other Arab countries and on May 22 Nasser announced that the Straits of Tiran were closed to Israeli shipping. Four days later he publicly declared that he intended to destroy Israel, and military contingents from other Arab states began to arrive in Egypt.

The lead-up to war

Israel now turned to the Western powers for support in having the Straits of Tiran reopened. France expressed some muted sympathy, but was at the time trying to improve her relations with the Arab countries. Britain and the United States were more positive in their support, but with the Soviet Union supporting the Arabs, they were not prepared for a military confrontation with her in the Middle East. Instead, they tried to bring world opinion on to the Israeli side.

To the Israelis it seemed increasingly that the longer they waited the more overwhelming the Arab military strength against them would become. There seemed no answer but to attack first.

The Six-Day War

Early on the morning of June 5, 1967, Israeli aircraft struck Egyptian airfields. Within a few hours most of the Egyptian Air Force had been destroyed on the ground. At midday Jordanian, Syrian and Iraqi aircraft attacked Israeli targets. In turn, their airfields were also attacked by the Israeli Air Force with such success that by the end of the first day it had air supremacy.

On the ground, Israeli armored columns, after some fierce fighting, broke through the Egyptian defenses in Sinai and, as in 1956, raced for the Canal. Unlike in 1956, Israel was also fighting on two other fronts. She had hoped that Jordan would stay out of the fighting, but on that first morning Nasser telephoned the King claiming that he had destroyed many Israeli aircraft and that his tanks were moving to link up with the Jordanians. Hussein therefore gave the order to attack, which his forces began to do south of Jerusalem.

The Israelis immediately launched attacks of their own. By the end of June 7 they had seized the Arab half of Jerusalem, after fierce fighting, and occupied the west bank of the Jordan River. King Hussein himself was very bitter. The Syrians and Iraqis had promised to send troops to help him, but neither had done so.

Syria had been more cautious than her two allies. Rather than attack the Israelis she merely shelled Israeli territory. The Israelis themselves, busy on the other two fronts, were content to do little until they had dealt with Egypt and Jordan. On June 9, however, having secured the east bank of the Suez Canal and defeated the Jordanians, they attacked the Syrian positions in the Golan Heights which had for so long dominated Israeli territory north of the Sea of Galilee. Within 24 hours they had broken through and pursued the Syrians back to and beyond Kuneitra.

ISRAEL'S TERRITORIAL GAINS AFTER THE SIX-DAY WAR

MEDITERRANEAN SEA

TEL AVIV • — WEST BANK / Jordan River
JERUSALEM
PORT SAID — GAZA •
I S R A E L
CAIRO • — SUEZ •
JORDAN
S I N A I
EILAT • AQABA
E G Y P T — Gulf of Suez — GULF OF AQABA
SAUDI ARABIA

■ Israeli territory in June 1967
▨ Israeli territory after June 1967

0 Km — 160
0 Miles — 100

RED SEA

Arab defeat

The United Nations had not been idle. On the first day of fighting they had unanimously called for a ceasefire, and repeated it on the next day. On the 7th, Israel (having achieved her objectives), Jordan and Egypt (because they had had enough) agreed to it. Israel and Syria would not at first agree to the United Nations demand, but once the Golan Heights had been captured, both accepted it. The United Nations Truce Supervision Organization (UNTSO) was deployed to make sure that it held on all fronts.

In 1956 Israel had been prepared to withdraw to her prewar frontiers. Now she refused to do so, arguing that she needed buffer zones to protect her from Arab attacks in the future. She effectively tripled in size and gained easily defendable frontiers. With her newly won territory she also took over the 1,500,000 Gaza Strip and West Bank Palestinians. Would she now be able to control them better within her frontiers and how would her Arab neighbors react to the humiliation of their defeat? As Egypt, Syria and Jordan had all lost national territory, including holy Islamic places, the chances of peace in the future seemed virtually non-existent.

A Palestinian refugee camp in Amman, Jordan.

CHAPTER 3

THE SUPERPOWERS STEP IN

The territorial gains made by Israel in 1967 left surrounding Arab countries intent upon revenge. In 1973, Egypt and Syria, with Soviet backing, tried to force Israel to withdraw to its previous borders in one of the most violent wars of the modern period. When that failed, Egypt tried a different approach, using the United States to help gain a peace treaty with the Israelis. Other Arabs, particularly the Palestinians, favored a more violent solution, including the use of terrorism.

The 1967 Arab-Israeli war did not solve any existing problems but merely added to them. Not only was the situation of the Palestinians made worse, but Israel was now occupying Jordanian, Syrian and Egyptian territory. The loss of her oil wells in Sinai and drying up of Suez Canal revenues caused severe economic hardship for Egypt. Matters were made more difficult by the fact that increasingly the Middle East seemed to be an area for superpower rivalry.

The United States, largely thanks to a strong domestic Jewish lobby, became even more determined in her support for Israel and refused to back United Nations resolutions calling on her to withdraw from her newly occupied territories. This threw the Arabs even more into the arms of the Soviet Union and the Eastern Bloc and they quickly replaced the weaponry which Egypt had lost in the recent war.

A summit conference of Arab states held at Khartoum, capital of Sudan, in September 1967 resolved that: the richer oil states would give annual financial aid to Egypt and Jordan; none of the rights of the Palestinians would be given up; and no peace treaty with Israel would be made. Further fighting in the Middle East seemed inevitable. Indeed, from July 1967 onwards there were constant clashes between the Arab and Israeli armed forces especially along the banks of the Suez Canal.

Resolution 242

In early November 1967 the Security Council of the United Nations met to consider three resolutions on the Middle East. After much negotiation, a British compromise resolution, based on the UN Charter principle that no country should occupy or seize territory by force of arms, was unanimously adopted. In essence it called for the withdrawal of Israeli forces from all territory occupied as a result of the 1967 war.

In return, all states in the region were to recognize each other's sovereignty, independence and territorial integrity and were to live at peace with one another. A special UN representative was appointed to go to the Middle East to put this into effect through negotiation. Resolution 242, as it was called, marked a big step forward and there was very real hope that at last the problems of the Middle East could be solved.

While there was a marked lull in the border clashes as a result of the adoption of Resolution 242, the resolution did nothing for the Palestinians, apart from calling for a "just settlement to the refugee problem." The PLO, now based in camps in Jordan and Lebanon, remained determined to regain its homeland.

Cross-border guerrilla attacks on Israeli targets and Israeli retaliation continued. In summer 1968, however, these PLO attacks took on a new form with the decision to attack Israeli targets abroad. The first incident occurred in July when the PLO seized an Israeli airliner in Algeria. Aircraft hijackings quickly became a major weapon of terrorists all over the world.

War in Oman

The Arabian Peninsula was another scene of conflict with Soviet backed guerrillas from South Yemen (formerly Aden) determined to push through Oman and secure the oil-rich sheikdoms in the southeast corner of the peninsula. Their cause was helped by the Sultan of Oman, who denied his people education and kept them firmly under his control.

By 1970 it seemed as though the Yemenis would achieve their aim, but in July the Sultan was over-thrown by his English-educated son Qabus. He immediately began to introduce reforms and asked for British help. Teams of military advisers were quickly sent in and the tide began to turn. Nevertheless, it was not until 1975 that Oman was finally pacified.

Meanwhile the border war in Sinai rumbled on. PLO attacks increased, as did Israeli retaliation. This caused a dilemma for Nasser. The Israeli strikes on PLO bases in Jordan and Lebanon inevitably brought the citizens of both countries into the firing line. The governments of both countries increasingly resented this, as they could not exercise any control over PLO activities.

Black September

In Jordan the situation became extremely serious. By late summer 1970, it seemed as if some sections of the PLO, using Jordanian bases, were trying to provoke the Israelis into occupying more Arab territory. This would then force the Arab states to attack Israel. King Hussein became convinced that the PLO was also trying to engineer his overthrow. In early September 1970 the PLO hijacked no less than four civil airliners, three of which they forced to land in Jordan and then destroyed. International reaction was fierce and this gave Hussein the excuse to disarm the PLO, but they refused to hand over their weapons. The Jordanian Army attacked them and the Syrian Army moved in to support the PLO.

After much discussion it was President Nasser, by now a sick man, who defused the crisis. The Syrians withdrew from Jordan and a ceasefire between the Jordanian Army and PLO was arranged. The PLO had suffered heavy casualties in the fighting of "Black September," as it became known, and the result was that the organization moved to Lebanon. It cost Nasser his last reserves of strength and on September 27 he died, deeply mourned by his country and the whole Arab world. His place was taken by Vice-President Anwar el-Sadat.

Sadat comes to power

Sadat was little known to the world at large and many people, especially the Israelis and Americans, believed that Nasser's death would create a vacuum. Sadat, however, was equally determined to bring about a lasting peace, but not at the expense of abandoning Arab territory or the Palestinian cause.

Throughout this time the United Nations repre-sentative in the Middle East, Gunnar Jarring, had continued his efforts to get Resolution 242 im-plemented. A ceasefire was finally put into effect on July 1, 1970, marking the end of the Sinai border war. However, the PLO was not a party to the ceasefire and continued to mount attacks on Israel.

Ceasefire problems

While extensions of the ceasefire were agreed, there was little progress towards a political solution. The main sticking point was still Israel's belief that Egypt would not honor any peace treaty once the Israeli forces had withdrawn from the occupied territories.

At the beginning of 1971 a first step was proposed: to get the Suez Canal reopened. To accomplish this, Israel would have to pull back her forces from the east bank, but she was not prepared to allow the Canal to be outside the range of her artillery. Thus the idea came to nothing. Within the United States there was continued suspicion of Soviet motives in Egypt and a hardening of support for Israel. The Soviets, in fact, intended to remove their military advisers from Egypt once a settlement had been reached.

Rearming the Egyptians

By now the Egyptian armed forces had been re-equipped with Soviet weapons. Most important of these were air defense missiles. The power of the Israeli Air Force had been decisive in 1967 but these missiles meant that Egypt could now counter it. Although Sadat knew that Israel could not be defeated in open battle, the improvement of Egypt's military position and the political deadlock convinced him by the end of 1971 that the only way forward was to attack Israel. If Egypt could score an early success and win worldwide support, then Israel might be forced to withdraw from the occupied territories.

He still needed more Soviet arms to achieve this, especially since in February 1972 US President Richard Nixon authorized further deliveries of combat aircraft to Israel. Nixon hoped this would ensure him the Jewish vote in the presidential election being held that year. The Soviets, however, not wanting to be drawn into a major confrontation with the United States in the Middle East, would not support Egyptian military action against Israel. They wanted to wait and see the result of the US presidential election, which was to be held in November 1972.

President Nixon was meanwhile trying to balance the additional arms supplies to Israel with friendly approaches to Egypt. Sadat was encouraged by this. He also realized that he needed the support of the Arab League. This meant not just providing military forces, but also money. The oil-rich countries of the League, who had the money, were, like the Americans, suspicious of the Soviet presence in Egypt and were unwilling to give support while it remained there.

Egypt expels the Soviets

For these reasons, in July 1972 President Sadat ordered the Soviets to remove their advisers from Egypt. This move took the world by surprise, especially the Soviets and Americans. The Soviets, with war clouds threatening, were relieved in some ways, because they did not want their pilots and other military advisers to be directly involved in a conflict with Israel. This was very likely to draw the United States into the fighting.

The Soviets departed, however, with some ill will, which did not prevent them from continuing to provide Egypt with arms. The United States, on the other hand, took no steps to improve relations with Egypt.

The Lod airport massacre

In May 1972, 26 innocent civilians were massacred at Lod airport in Israel. A further 72 people were also wounded in the incident. Those who carried out the attack turned out to be Japanese terrorists working for the PLO.

This showed that the PLO was now part of an international terrorist network and that it was not just Israeli citizens who were in the firing line. In the light of these acts it is hardly surprising that the United States remained unfriendly towards Egypt, a firm supporter of the PLO.

The PLO itself had undergone a split. The main body, under Yasser Arafat, was still dedicated to attacking targets in Israel. During the late 1960s, however, more politically minded leftist Palestinian groups began to break away and form "splinter groups." Most prominent of these was the Popular Front for the Liberation of Palestine (PFLP) led by Dr George Habash.

It was these groups which were forging links with terrorists in Europe and Japan. In September 1972 one of them – Black September – killed 11 Israeli athletes at the Munich Olympics.

The lead-up to war

During the remainder of 1972 and 1973, Egypt worked to mobilize the resources of the Arab League against Israel and the results were encouraging, with all members pledging financial and/or military support. Under great secrecy, preparations for the coming war were made. At the same time, Egypt continued to make friendly overtures towards the United States, but no progress was made.

The Israeli view was that Egypt had lost the will to fight and that her position on the east bank of the Suez

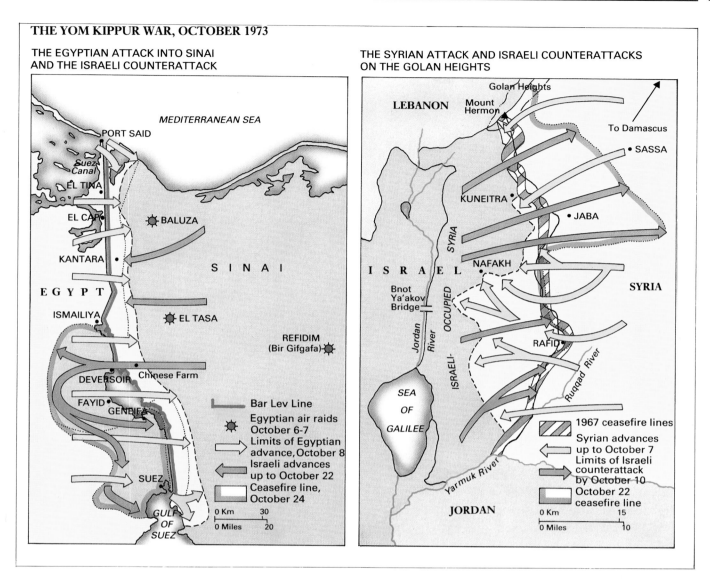

THE YOM KIPPUR WAR, OCTOBER 1973

THE EGYPTIAN ATTACK INTO SINAI
AND THE ISRAELI COUNTERATTACK

THE SYRIAN ATTACK AND ISRAELI COUNTERATTACKS
ON THE GOLAN HEIGHTS

Canal was secure. Indeed, there was little military activity on the Canal and the Egyptians launched a very clever campaign of misinformation, pretending that their armed forces were ill-prepared and poorly equipped. The effectiveness of this campaign was shown on October 6, 1973.

The Yom Kippur War

President Sadat chose October 6 to strike for two reasons. First, the tides in the Suez Canal were favorable for a crossing. More important, it was Yom Kippur Day, the "Day of Atonement," a Jewish fast day and a national holiday. The Israelis would be unlikely to be prepared for an attack.

Preceded by air strikes on Israeli airfields in Sinai and a short, sharp, but massive artillery and rocket bombardment, Egyptian forces crossed the Canal in no less than 10 places in the early afternoon of the 6th.

The Egyptians breach the sand banks along the Suez Canal.

It was a skillfully planned and well-rehearsed operation, using high-pressure hoses to breach the canal banks and Soviet-supplied pontoon bridges to cross the water. The attackers were soon through the fortified Bar Lev Line. At the same time, the Syrians launched their tanks against the Israeli positions on the Golan Heights.

Although the Israelis were taken by surprise, they were able to mobilize their reserves quickly. Even so, for the first three days they were under much pressure. Some of the strongpoints on the Bar Lev Line held out for days, but others were quickly overrun. The Egyptians soon established a number of sizable bridgeheads on the east bank of the Suez Canal. The Israeli Air Force could make little impression on these as the bridgeheads were well defended by surface-to-air missiles (SAMs).

The Israelis did have tanks in reserve behind the Bar Lev Line, but it was not until the third day (8th) that they counterattacked. When they did so, they suffered heavy casualties from Egyptian portable anti-tank guided weapons (ATGW).

Fighting on the Golan Heights

On the Israeli-Syrian front the situation for the Israelis quickly became as serious as it was on the Suez Canal. While the Syrians gained little ground in the northern part of the Golan Heights, farther south they managed to break through and by midnight on October 7 their forces had almost reached the Jordan River. If they crossed this they would be entering the heart of Israel.

The Israelis now launched fierce counterattacks. After three days of desperate fighting, the Israelis managed to regain the Golan Heights. They now began to drive into Syria and looked as though they might even reach the capital, Damascus. At this point, Iraqi and Jordanian forces attacked the southern flank of the Israeli penetration and the Syrians also launched attacks in the center and north. Gradually the Israeli attack was slowed and then halted.

The Sinai Front

Meanwhile, in Sinai the Israelis had concluded that the only way in which they could counter the Egyptian seizure of the east bank of the Canal was to cross it themselves and occupy Egyptian territory. They could only do this, however, if the Egyptians were weakened. Their chance came when, in response to desperate calls for aid from Syria, the Egyptians abandoned their previous strategy and tried to advance beyond their ATGW/SAM defenses into Sinai.

The climax came on October 14 when no less than 2,000 tanks were locked in battle in Sinai, the biggest tank action since 1943. By the end of the day the Egyptian armor had withdrawn, having suffered heavy casualties. The time had come for the Israelis to launch their counterblow. This mounted late on the afternoon of October 15. The plan was to cross the Canal just

A Soviet supplied T-62 tank abandoned on the Golan Heights following the fighting in October 1973.

north of the Great Bitter Lake. During heavy fighting overnight the Israelis managed to establish a toehold on the west bank in the early hours of the 16th.

During the next few days the Israelis slowly enlarged their bridgehead, threatening Ismailiya in the north and more seriously, Suez in the south. Even more serious for the Egyptians was that the southern thrust had by midday on the 21st almost cut off the Egyptian Third Army, the southern of the two armies which had made the attack across the Canal, from its supply lines on the west bank.

Moves towards a ceasefire

The destruction of weaponry on both sides had been enormous and both the United States and Soviet Union had been flying in arms to make good these losses. Syria was thought to have lost almost 900 tanks in the first three days of fighting. The United Nations had from the outset called for a ceasefire, but the Arabs would only agree to this if Israel voluntarily withdrew to the pre-June 1967 borders. Israel, especially now that she was at war, refused to consider this.

It was, however, the Soviet Union which took the first positive steps towards bringing an end to the fighting. The Israeli recovery and her drives into Syria and across the Suez Canal were worrying the Soviet leader, Leonid Brezhnev.

He therefore asked President Nixon if his National Security Adviser, Henry Kissinger, could fly to Moscow and see him. The two agreed on a joint demand for a ceasefire, but linked to peace talks. They now informed Egypt and Israel, who were both suspicious.

Nevertheless, on the morning of October 22, UN Security Council Resolution No. 338 called for a ceasefire by both sides within 12 hours. On the Syrian front, where the Israeli attacks had been halted, this was accepted and it came into effect. The Israelis, however, were determined to cut off the Egyptian Third Army and seize as much Egyptian territory as they could and so improve their bargaining position. The Egyptians thus had no option but to continue fighting.

President Sadat now asked both the Soviet Union and the United States to send in troops to ensure that the Israelis withdrew to the line reached on October 22. President Nixon rejected this, while Brezhnev said that he was not prepared to act on his own. Concerned by the increasing tension, Nixon now put his forces on nuclear alert on the 25th, but on the same day another ceasefire resolution was put to the UN Security Council and agreed. A UN force would be sent to supervise the ceasefire.

The oil embargo

On that same day a new dimension was added to the Middle East conflict. The Organization of Arab Petroleum Exporting Countries (OAPEC) declared that it was raising the price of its oil by 70 per cent and placing a boycott on supplies of those countries giving active support to Israel.

This brought home how dependent Western industrialized countries were on Middle East oil. The result was that oil prices skyrocketed overnight and some countries introduced rationing for the first time in years. By January 1974 oil prices were four times higher than they had been four months earlier.

The United States steps in

In the meantime, the UN peace-keeping forces began to arrive on October 27. It was, however, the Americans who persuaded the Israelis to accept the ceasefire. The Arabs now began to recognize that the United States was the only country which Israel would listen to. As a result, the United States began to take an increasingly dominant role in the Middle East at the expense of the Soviets. As for President Sadat, although militarily the Arabs came off worse, he did achieve his aim of getting the peace process moving.

The first step was to get the Israelis to withdraw to the positions they reached on October 22, but in spite of Henry Kissinger's efforts the Israelis were extremely slow, even though exchanges of prisoners of war did start quickly.

The Western powers believed that the only way forward was to convene a peace conference and proposed that it should be held at Geneva, Switzerland, scene of many such meetings in the past. While Egypt was prepared to attend, Syria was not, unless the aim of the conference was clearly stated: Israel's withdrawal from all occupied territories.

Eventually at the end of December the conference took place under the supervision of the UN Secretary-General and with the United States, Soviet Union, Egypt, Jordan and Israel attending. However, it failed to reach any agreement.

In January 1974, Kissinger managed to achieve an agreement between Israel and Egypt for the Israeli withdrawal from the west bank of the Canal. The opposing forces on both sides would be reduced and UN troops would act as a buffer between them.

Egyptian isolation

The increasing American influence in the peace process resulted in a rift between the Soviet Union and Egypt. The Soviets had undertaken to deliver more arms to Egypt to make good their losses in the October War. Now, jealous of the growing relationship between Kissinger and Sadat and feeling that they were being left out of the negotiations, they cancelled the arms shipments.

Egypt also had problems with Syria. Relations had been soured over the Geneva Conference, which Syria felt was ineffective in achieving Israeli withdrawals from her territory. Indeed, Israel refused not only to give up the Golan Heights, but also to withdraw from the town of Kuneitra, which she had overrun during the 1967 war.

While other Arab countries were prepared to lift the oil embargo on the United States, Syria, supported by Libya, was not. Nonetheless, in March 1974 the embargo was lifted, although oil prices did not drop as a result. At the end of May, however, again largely through Kissinger's efforts, an agreement between Israel and Syria was reached.

Palestinian recognition

The United States and the Soviet Union now stated that they were determined to secure a lasting peace in the Middle East on the basis of UN Resolution 242; Israel would have to withdraw from the occupied territories, and the Palestinians would have to have self-determination. In the meantime the Arab countries had agreed between them that the PLO must attend any peace conference and they had also recognized Yasser Arafat as the Palestinian leader.

The next step was to gain international recognition of this. In November 1974, therefore, the Arab states proposed that Yasser Arafat be allowed to speak at the United Nations. This was opposed by the United States and Israel, but the motion was overwhelmingly carried by the UN General Assembly, and speak he did. It was also agreed that the PLO should have observer status at the United Nations. The Israeli reaction to this was that they would only negotiate with the PLO on the battlefield.

While significant steps had been taken during 1974 towards achieving a more stable situation in the Middle East, PLO attacks on Israeli targets had continued. In May 1974 there had been a tragic episode in the northern Galilee town of Maalot. PLO gunmen had taken the pupils of a school hostage. Israeli commandos stormed the school, killing the gunmen, but 22 children also lost their lives. The Israelis believed that no compromise could be reached with the PLO while they continued to commit atrocities.

Peace moves

Slowly the step-by-step peace process continued. In September 1975 a further agreement was signed at Geneva. The Israelis agreed to withdraw east of the key passes in Sinai, while Egypt pledged not to threaten force. To get Israel to do this, however, the United States had to promise her substantial arms deliveries and agree not to recognize the PLO or to enter into negotiations with it unless it agreed to accept Resolutions 242 or 338.

While this marked definite progress towards peace between Israel and Egypt, other Arab countries, especially Syria and Jordan, were not pleased. They objected to the exclusion of the PLO from the peace negotiations and the fact that the Israeli occupation of Jordanian and Syrian territory was not being addressed.

Syria now drew closer to the Soviet Union, who had stayed outside the 1975 Geneva Agreement. A number of non-aligned nations also forced a resolution through the UN General Assembly declaring that Zionism was like Fascism (the extreme right-wing, anti-communist doctrine which originated in Italy in the 1920s and 1930s). One bright spot was that an international naval force did succeed in clearing the Suez Canal of mines, war debris and other obstacles. The accumulated silt was also removed and the Canal was reopened to shipping in 1975.

The Lebanese Civil War

A further complication was Lebanon. On April 13, 1975, the veteran Lebanese Christian leader Pierre Gemayel was attacked in Beirut. Four of his bodyguards were killed. His Phalangist party followers retaliated by attacking a Palestinian bus going to a wedding party, killing 22 members of the PLO.

This marked the beginning of a civil war, which transformed the country. The increasing number of Palestinians in Lebanon were kept in camps by the authorities and denied many ordinary human rights. Between the Christians and Muslims in the Lebanon there had been an uneasy peace, but the Christians dominated the country. The Muslims increasingly saw the PLO as an ally, while the PLO saw in the Muslim Lebanese friends who would help it improve its position in the country.

Like any civil war, that in Lebanon was marked by atrocities committed by both sides. There were constant street battles in Beirut and worse, massacres of refugees in camps. Much of Beirut was destroyed. It lost its position as the financial center of the Middle East and its reputation as an international playground for the rich.

In June 1976, Syrian forces moved into northern Lebanon, fearful that if the PLO gained the upper hand it would prove to be an uncomfortable neighbor. When some sort of peace was finally restored in autumn 1976, the Syrians were left occupying much of northern Lebanon, while the PLO dominated the south. There seemed no solution in sight to the conflict.

New peace initiatives

At the end of 1976, the election of Jimmy Carter as US president gave fresh hope to the Arabs that peace might be established. In February 1977, Carter sent his

Street fighting in Lebanon, October 1975.
Inset: *Extensive bomb damage in Beirut, 1975.*

Secretary of State, Cyrus Vance, on a tour of the Middle East capitals armed with a new proposal, which seemed likely to produce results.

In return for phased withdrawals by Israel from the occupied territories, the Palestinian right to self-determination would be recognized in the form of a separate state or federation with Jordan. The PLO would, however, have to accept Israel's sovereignty and integrity, but the United States recognized the PLO's right to be represented in the talks.

The Entebbe raid

While the Arab states accepted these proposals, Israel maintained her opposition to PLO representation. As far as she was concerned, continuing PLO terrorist activities made this impossible. This was reinforced in June 1976, when four terrorists, two from the West German Baader-Meinhof Gang and two from the Popular Front for the Liberation of Palestine (PFLP), hijacked an Air France plane. It had 250 passengers, including 96 Israelis, on board.

The terrorists forced the aircraft to land at Entebbe, Uganda, and demanded the release of 53 convicted terrorists – 40 held in Israel and the others in European and Kenyan jails – in exchange for the hostages' lives. Negotiations over the release of the hostages became deadlocked and the Israelis sent a special forces team by air to Entebbe.

In a spectacular operation, the Israeli troops succeeded in killing the terrorists – now numbering 13, having been reinforced by further PFLP members at Entebbe. They rescued the hostages, most of whom were unharmed. Some 35 Ugandan soldiers who tried to resist were also killed.

Sadat goes to Israel

There was now a renewed effort on the part of the United States and the Soviet Union to set up another conference in Geneva involving all interested parties. The problem of the PLO and its recognition remained. On November 9, 1977 President Sadat astounded the world by announcing that he was prepared to debate the matter with the Israelis in their parliament, the Knesset. A week later an ivitation came from Israeli prime minister Menachem Begin, via Washington, for Sadat to visit Jerusalem.

In spite of warnings from President Assad of Syria that there would be a violent Arab reaction, Sadat accepted the invitation. While Sadat made it clear that the visit did not mean that Egypt was aiming for a separate peace with Israel or any recognition of Israel's right to remain in any of the occupied territories, the visit resulted in a gap between Egypt and the other Arab states. Thus, when Sadat invited all parties to a conference in Cairo in December only Israel, the United States and the United Nations sent representatives. The other Arab countries and the Soviet Union refused to attend.

The hostages return home to Israel following the Entebbe raid in July 1976. Following a brilliant rescue mission executed by Israeli paratroops, most of the hostages were able to fly home immediately.

Deadlock

Nevertheless, Israel and Egypt did form a committee, which met in Jerusalem in January 1978 in order to try and keep the momentum of negotiations going. This broke down in March, when Israel, increasingly angered by PLO attacks from bases inside Lebanon, carried out a military operation designed to destroy those bases.

The United Nations acted quickly, sending yet another peace-keeping force to the Middle East, the United Nations Interim Force in Lebanon (UNIFIL). UNIFIL was to ensure the Israeli withdrawal, which took place in June, hand back effective authority in the area to the Lebanese government and prevent the region from being used for hostile operations.

Egypt tried to improve her relations with Syria without success. Attempts to call an Arab summit conference also failed. The situation seemed to be totally deadlocked.

The Camp David agreement

In August 1978 President Carter invited both Sadat and Begin to meet him at his holiday retreat in the United States, Camp David. Both accepted, although few of the other Arab states supported the idea, believing that it would end in failure. After 12 days of intense discussion a draft agreement was drawn up and in March 1979 Egypt and Israel signed a historic, formal peace treaty. This was a triumph for American policy in the Middle East and was a welcome boost for President Carter's reputation.

This marked the end of 30 years of being in a state of war with one another. The treaty provided for a three-stage withdrawal by Israel of her armed forces and civilians from Sinai to the original Egypt-Palestine border, excluding the Gaza Strip. In return Egypt guaranteed free passage of Israeli shipping through the Suez Canal and declared the Straits of Tiran and Gulf of Aqaba international waterways. The Egypt-Israel peace treaty was the most positive step towards solving the problems of the Middle East since 1948. It was, however, only a step and had done little to address the issues of Israel's continued occupation of other Arab territory and, more fundamentally, the plight of the Palestinians. The situation, too, was now to be complicated by other, new factors.

President Jimmy Carter, flanked by President Anwar el-Sadat and Prime Minister Menachem Begin, at the signing of the Camp David agreement, September 1978.

An anti-Shah demonstration in Iran, 1978.

CHAPTER 4
HOLY WAR

Arab-Israeli conflict did not cease following the Camp David agreement, but it was overshadowed by the growth of religious rivalries within the Muslim world. The rise of fundamentalism in Iran sent shock waves throughout countries ruled by more moderate followers of Islam, and produced a costly war in the Gulf between Iran and Iraq. As this coincided with continued violence in Lebanon, fueled by outside interference, the chances of peace seemed slim indeed.

On January 16, 1979, Mohammed Reza Pahlavi, Shah of Iran, was to leave his country, never to return. Two weeks later the Ayatollah Khomeini would fly into the capital Tehran from Paris to a rapturous welcome from his fellow countrymen. This upheaval would quickly produce another area of unrest and serve to compound the problems of the Middle East.

The crisis had its origins in 1953, when Prime Minister Mossadeq had fled from Iran. One of the results of this revolution had been a gradual takeover of Iranian oil interests by Western oil companies, and thereafter the country had slipped into corruption as its economic situation grew worse and worse.

The Shah's rule

The country became more and more dependent on US financial aid. The Shah considered that the only way to put his country back on its feet was to institute drastic reforms in order to modernize it and make it more self-sufficient.

He relied on Western-educated technocrats whose outlook was often in direct opposition to the country's Islamic traditions. Determined to force through his reform program, the Shah gradually became increasingly dictatorial, relying on the hated secret police, the SAVAK. Yet the vast majority of his people supported him, as a 1963 referendum (vote) showed.

Islamic opposition

Many of the religious leaders, including the Ayatollah, did not support the new ideas. They were especially shocked by the adoption of Western dress in public by many of the better-off women. This ran totally against the spirit of Islam, which lays down that a woman must never display her beauty in public. In Iran, the *chowdah*, a black head-to-foot shapeless garment covering all but the face, had been the traditional form of female dress, so the effect on the religious leaders of photographs of the Shah's wife in a bikini may be imagined.

Khomeini himself was exiled in 1963 for opposing the Shah's rule. He went for a short time to Turkey, then traveled to Iraq, a Sunni-ruled country with a long history of enmity towards the Aryan, predominantly Shi'ite, population of Iran. Many religious leaders and others who opposed the Shah's government joined Khomeini in Iraq, where he was to remain until October 1978.

Nevertheless, the Shah's reforms did bring increasing prosperity to the middle classes, although the standard of living of the poor (who also tended to be the people with the strongest Shi'ite beliefs) remained virtually unaltered. As a deep divide began to open up between the rulers and the ruled, some sort of revolution became inevitable.

The Shah sits on the "peacock" throne, 1967.

Oil riches

The rise in oil prices in 1973-74 made Iran one of the richest countries in the Middle East and increased the Shah's sense of power. He wanted his country to be a major force in the politics of the region and to this end he created very strong armed forces, equipped with the latest Western weapons. It was this ambition, coupled with a strong policy of anti-communism, that prompted him to send an Imperial Iranian Battle Group to help the Sultan of Oman in 1973, when the latter was under threat from pro-Marxist guerrillas.

In spite of Iran's growing riches, by the second half of the 1970s she was, like most other industrialized or semi-industrialized states, suffering from increasing inflation. The Shah's answer was a freeze on borrowing money, bringing a halt to certain developments which might have benefited the people and further fueling their displeasure.

The Shah's fall

Support for the Ayatollah Khomeini and his strong religious convictions grew, particularly as more and more Iranians saw the increasing Western influence on the country as an insult to Islam. By autumn 1978, civil unrest had become commonplace.

At the Shah's request, the Iraqi President, Saddam Hussein, expelled Khomeini, who promptly moved to Paris and began to incite rebellion against the Shah. Iran soon became virtually ungovernable: in the end it seemed as though only the Shah's own household troops, the Imperial Guard, remained loyal to him. He had little choice but to flee the country.

The Ayatollah comes to power

When the Ayatollah Khomeini took over the country in February 1979 he declared that he would rid it of all Western influences. One of his first acts was to remove Iran from the Central Treaty Organization (CENTO), the pro-Western defense alliance established in 1959. At the same time, Iranian women were ordered to put the *chowdah* back on and anyone who was suspected of having any connection with the Shah was thrown into prison or executed.

Many upper and middle class people fled the country. Iran quickly came under the grip of Khomeini's fanatical young followers, the Revolutionary Guards. To Western eyes it seemed as if the country was falling apart, especially as the early stages of the revolution caused a dramatic drop in the production of Iranian oil.

The Iranian Hostage crisis

Anti-Western feeling intensified, culminating in November 1979 when so-called Iranian "students" stormed the US Embassy in Tehran, taking 52 members of the diplomatic staff hostage and demanding the return of the Shah from exile to face trial for crimes against the people. Although this was a flagrant violation of international law, which protects diplomats, the United States appeared powerless to do anything about it.

With no armed forces closer than the Mediterranean, a quick response was out of the question. Even if some sort of rescue mission had been possible, the consequences could have been catastrophic, particularly in terms of an extension of conflict within the Middle East or between the superpowers.

In the end, when negotiations had failed and the United States had moved naval forces into the Gulf of Oman, a rescue mission (Operation Eagle Claw) was attempted in April 1980, but by then it was too late. Because of the immense distances involved and the need for complete surprise, Delta Force commandos had to evolve an elaborate plan which depended on equipment (especially helicopters) which proved unable to cope with desert conditions. Once this had failed, the United States had to accept humiliating

Iranian students demand the return of the Shah, 1980.

terms for the release of their diplomats: as the Shah was by now dead, the only terms acceptable to the Ayatollah involved the releasing of Iranian assets, frozen as part of President Carter's response to the overthrow of the Shah. The hostages returned to the United States in January 1981.

Islamic fundamentalism

It was not only the United States which was affected by the upheavals in Iran. In the same month as the US hostages were seized, there was a terrorist incident in Saudi Arabia's Mecca, the holiest city in the Muslim world. Some Islamic extremists ran amok in the Grand Mosque and killed a number of innocent pilgrims. Behind their action was a message from Iran that all Muslims must return to the traditional code of Islam.

This became known as "Islamic fundamentalism" and its growth threatened a number of interests in the Middle East. Because Western influence was seen by the Ayatollah as a prime element in the weakening of Islam, any growth of fundamentalism obviously affected the West, but the ripples went wider than that. The Soviet Union, with a substantial Muslim minority in its southern states, also feared the spread of new ideas which ran counter to those of communism, while a number of Middle East countries, ruled by or containing large populations of Sunni Muslims, viewed the growth of Shi'ite influence with concern. In some of the smaller Gulf States, where the Sunni rulers were aware that their positions were dependent on support from predominantly Shi'ite populations, the fear was acute; so much so that in 1981 they, together with Saudi Arabia, formed the Gulf Cooperation Council (GCC) for mutual protection.

The invasion of Afghanistan

Further complications arose during Christmas 1979. Soviet troops invaded Afghanistan, deposing the head of state and inserting a man loyal to Moscow. Afghanistan has always been a fiercely independent country and many Afghans, viewing Soviet-inspired communism as a threat to Islam, resisted and have continued to resist to the present day. More importantly, to the West at least, the invasion implied a renewed Soviet interest in the Middle East, for although Afghanistan itself is theoretically outside the region, it borders directly onto Iran, with its oilfields and access to the "warm-water ports" of the Gulf. As with the Iranian hostages, however, there was little the West could do except voice its disgust.

Iran-Iraq tension

The situation was made much worse by the growing tensions between Iran and Iraq – tensions which led to all-out war in September 1980. Many of these arose from the ethnic and religious differences between the two countries, but these were fueled by other, more precise problems in the 1970s. Chief among these was a territorial dispute over the exact border between Iran and Iraq close to the tip of the Gulf.

Since Turkish times, the border had been laid down along the east bank of the Shatt al Arab waterway, meaning that Iraq had full control of that route, forcing the Iranians to pay tolls on their oil shipments from Abadan and Khorramshahr, while threatening the closure of the waterway in the event of crisis or war. Iran had complained about this for some time, calling for a revised border along the center of the Shatt al Arab, with an Iraqi passage along the western half and an Iranian one along the eastern.

Iraq opposed such a settlement, but was forced to rethink its position in the mid-1970s when Iran gave increased support to Kurdish guerrillas fighting for national independence in the northern mountains of Iraq. By 1975, as Iranian expertise and arms were helping the Kurds to achieve some success, the Iraqis agreed to a deal: if the Iranians would stop their support to the rebels, Iraq would reconsider its stance regarding the Shatt al Arab. Just such an agreement was signed in Algiers in 1975; almost immediately, as the Kurds lost their support, the Iraqis regained control of their northern provinces, but the cost had been high.

The new Iran-Iraq border, down the center of the Shatt al Arab, restricted Iraqi access to the Gulf and denied them a potentially powerful weapon in their confrontation with Iran, a confrontation made much worse once the Shah had been overthrown. Iraq demanded the return of the Abu Musa and Tarib Islands. Add to this a deep personal hatred between the Ayatollah and Saddam Hussein (the former had not forgiven the Iraqi president for expelling him in 1978), and the ingredients for a war were clearly present.

Kurdish guerrillas have continued to fight for self-determination in the 1980s. They have used the Iran-Iraq war as an opportunity to regain control of parts of northern Iraq.

The Gulf War

The war between Iran and Iraq began in September 1980, at a time when Saddam Hussein was convinced that the Ayatollah's regime was weak. Iran was isolated from Western support because of the US Embassy seizure and many of its pro-Shah army and air force officers had been "purged." It seemed incapable of responding to a sudden attack across the Shatt al Arab which destroyed the Iranian oil refineries at Abadan and Khorramshahr.

Thus, when Iraqi troops attacked on September 22, most experts expected the war to be short and to result in a victory for Saddam Hussein. Indeed, during the first few weeks, as Iraqi forces seized Abadan and laid siege to Khorramshahr, this seemed to be the case.

But the fighting soon degenerated into a stalemate. Far from the Iranians being too weak to continue, the Iraqi assault acted as a focus for religious and nationalist feeling. Military officers returned from exile to fight for their country and the emotional appeal of fundamentalism ensured the Ayatollah virtually unlimited recruits, many of whom were convinced that to die in battle against the "great Satan" Saddam Hussein would guarantee them entry into Heaven. Very quickly, the superior weaponry and organization of the Iraqi forces were offset by the sheer weight of Iranian numbers. Khorramshahr fell to Iraq, but only at great cost, and the fighting on all fronts became an attritional affair, reminiscent of the First World War.

The war continues

During the second half of 1981, the Iranians had recovered sufficiently to mount counterattacks using massive "human-wave" assaults. By March 1982, the Iraqis had been forced to pull back to their pre-war border, since when they have been fighting for their

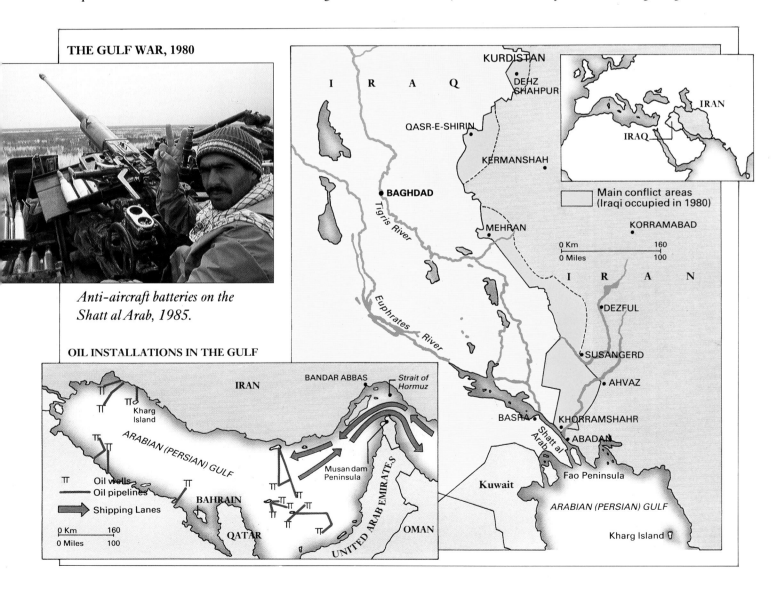

THE GULF WAR, 1980

Anti-aircraft batteries on the Shatt al Arab, 1985.

OIL INSTALLATIONS IN THE GULF

own territory. In the process, the Iraqis have used all the weapons at their disposal, including chemical agents and air attacks on Iranian cities. Casualties have risen alarmingly – some sources cite over a million dead altogether – and successive Iranian offensives have gradually increased the pressure on Saddam Hussein's regime.

In 1986, an Iranian attack across the Shatt al Arab almost cut the Iraqis off from access to the Gulf, while renewed Kurdish activity in the north, backed once again by Iran, threatened oil pipelines running west to outlets in the Mediterranean. If Saddam Hussein should lose the ability to ship oil out, his economy would probably collapse and he would be forced to sue for terms – terms which would include massive Iraqi payments to Iran for having started the war, the possible loss of the Shatt al Arab and, most telling of all, the fall from power of Saddam Hussein himself.

Stalemate

The war has dragged on not only because of Iraqi weapons against Iranian numbers, but also because neither side has managed to attract the sort of outside support which would be decisive. Neither superpower is really interested in victory by either side – if Iran were to win, the spread of fundamentalism would threaten the future of many of the pro-Western Gulf States and cause disquiet among the Muslims in the Soviet Union. Similarly, if Iraq were to come out on top, Saddam Hussein would probably turn against Israel with renewed vigor, pursuing his dream of becoming undisputed leader of the Arab world, and this would worry both the United States (as a supporter of Israel) and the Soviets (as supporters of Iraq's main rival among the Arabs, Syria).

By the same token, the traditionally influential European powers are worried about the future of oil supplies from the Gulf, threatened since 1984, when the Iraqis began a deliberate policy of bombing any ship carrying oil from Iran. Although this does not mean that they support Iran (they too fear the effects of fundamentalism on the countries of the GCC), it does leave them in a position where they will lend support to neither side. In the end, it would appear that most countries in the wider world are quite prepared to let the two rivals fight it out until both are so exhausted that neither can pose a threat. The chances of an end to the fighting would seem remote. In fact with the attack on the American destroyer USS *Stark* in 1987 and the subsequent decision by President Reagan to allow

Helicopters airlift wounded Iranian soldiers, 1985.

GCC oil tankers to fly the American flag (thereby implying that any attack upon them constitutes an attack on the United States), the Gulf remains an area fraught with danger.

The spread of fundamentalism

The Gulf War has not been the only consequence of the growth of Islamic fundamentalism, for its effects have been felt throughout the Middle East. In Egypt, for example, there has been a resurgence of the Muslim Brotherhood, made stronger by the signing of the Camp David agreement. Supporters in Syria of the Muslim Brotherhood were behind a series of sectarian massacres and killings, which caused the government of President Assad much concern.

The most devastating of the Muslim Brotherhood's terrorist acts came in 1981. In October, while taking the salute at a military parade in Cairo, President Sadat was gunned down by soldiers taking part in the parade. His brave unilateral stand for peace in the Middle East had won the admiration of many in the world, but had made him some implacable enemies among his fellow countrymen as well as among Arabs.

Withdrawal from Sinai

Sadat was succeeded by Hosni Mubarak who declared himself determined to continue his predecessor's work towards permanent peace. He too recognized the continuing vital role which the United States had to play in the peace process and this drew the two countries even closer together.

At the same time, the Israeli withdrawal from Sinai proceeded smoothly, cementing the peace accord between Israel and Egypt. On April 25, 1982 the evacuation was completed, with Sinai being made a demilitarized zone supervised by a special multinational force. However, there were still no signs that the remainder of Resolution 242 would be implemented; indeed Israel appeared to be tightening its grip on the West Bank, Jerusalem and the Golan Heights. In the light of events in Lebanon, this was probably understandable.

Lebanese problems

Lebanon never really had time to recover from the effects of the 1975-76 civil war. The Christian President, Elias Sarkis, had great difficulty in controlling the various factions in his own party, let alone the myriad of other groups within his troubled country – the Druze (led by Walid Jumblatt from 1977, when his father, Kamal, was assassinated), the Muslim militias and the Palestinians.

The intervention of the Syrians in 1976 may have prevented a Christian defeat, but Assad's forces had not been withdrawn, remaining firmly in control in the strategic Beka'a Valley to the east of Beirut.

The Syrian position

The Syrians were careful not to confront the Israelis – they occupied positions to the north of the unofficial "Red Line" – but their presence did nothing to ease the internal problems of Lebanon. During the first half of 1978, the Christian militias, led by father and son Pierre and Bashir Gemayel, combined with the Lebanese Front to oppose the Syrians. Fierce fighting took place between the two in Beirut in the first week of July, with the Israelis siding with the Lebanese Front militia forces (although not to the extent of armed intervention).

The eventual result was that by the end of the year Beirut had been split into two: East Beirut became a Christian enclave, while West Beirut came under the control of the Muslims. The Lebanese government effectively lost control of the city.

Continuing unrest

The clashes did not end there. Throughout 1979 and 1980, Syrian and Lebanese Front forces fought for control of key positions, drawing the Israelis in so that Israeli and Syrian aircraft clashed over Beirut. In response, the Syrians began to deploy surface-to-air missile (SAM) batteries in the Beka'a Valley. These covered the area over Beirut, but also, by virtue of their "slant range" (that is, their ability to be fired outward instead of straight up in the air), threatened Israeli freedom of movement in the air to the south of the Red Line. Israel quite naturally objected to this, being prevented from attacking the SAMs only by pressure from the United States.

But this was not the most immediate problem facing the Israelis on their northern border. In the aftermath of the Syrian intervention in 1976, the PLO had pulled away from Beirut into camps in southern Lebanon, from where they could mount terrorist attacks on northern Galilee. In March 1978, in response to a PLO raid into northern Israel three days earlier, the Israelis mounted an invasion of southern Lebanon. Between 20,000 and 25,000 troops supported by tanks, artillery, aircraft and gunboats crossed the border. At the same time Israeli aircraft struck targets much farther north, such as the Palestinian camps at Sabra, Shatilla and Bourj Al-Baranjneh. But the Palestinians had declined to fight so the Israelis had been forced to withdraw.

UNIFIL had been deployed to create a buffer between the Israelis and the PLO, but at the same time the Israelis had tried to create another buffer to the south of the UNIFIL positions, using the Christian militias commanded by Major Saad Haddad. When he attempted to impose his authority in what became known as "Haddadland," he proved to be particularly ruthless against Muslim villages, actions which led to fighting in the area. As this coincided with a spread of fundamentalism among the Shi'ites of Lebanon, another element was added to the chaos of the country.

Operation Peace for Galilee

Such an unsettled situation on the northern border could not be tolerated by Israelis intent on security, by the use of force if necessary. As terrorist attacks increased, the Israelis lost all confidence in UNIFIL, blaming the UN troops for allowing PLO infiltration of the border, but the real worries began in mid-1982, when Palestinian attacks on Israeli targets in Europe implied a new campaign of international terror.

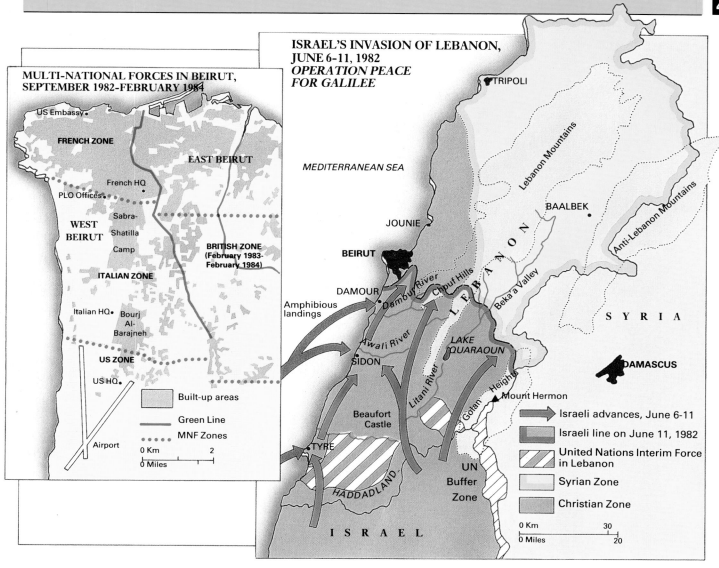

MULTI-NATIONAL FORCES IN BEIRUT, SEPTEMBER 1982–FEBRUARY 1984

US Embassy

FRENCH ZONE

EAST BEIRUT

French HQ

PLO Offices

Sabra-

WEST BEIRUT

Shatilla

Camp

BRITISH ZONE (February 1983–February 1984)

ITALIAN ZONE

Italian HQ

Bourj Al-Barajneh

US ZONE

US HQ

Airport

Built-up areas

Green Line

MNF Zones

0 Km 2

0 Miles

ISRAEL'S INVASION OF LEBANON, JUNE 6–11, 1982
OPERATION PEACE FOR GALILEE

TRIPOLI

MEDITERRANEAN SEA

Lebanon Mountains

JOUNIE

BAALBEK

Anti-Lebanon Mountains

BEIRUT

DAMOUR

Dambur River

Chouf Hills

Beka'a Valley

L E B A N O N

S Y R I A

Amphibious landings

Awali River

DAMASCUS

SIDON

LAKE QUARAOUN

Litani River

Golan Heights

Mount Hermon

Beaufort Castle

TYRE

UN Buffer Zone

Israeli advances, June 6–11

Israeli line on June 11, 1982

HADDADLAND

United Nations Interim Force in Lebanon

Syrian Zone

I S R A E L

Christian Zone

0 Km 30

0 Miles 20

These culminated in the attempted assassination of the Israeli ambassador to London, Shlomo Argov, on June 3. The Israelis responded by mounting air attacks on Palestinian camps in southern Lebanon, upon which the PLO started to fire rockets and artillery shells into *kibbutzim* in northern Galilee. On June 6, the Israelis decided to deal with the problem once and for all, committing massive forces to an all-out invasion of southern Lebanon – Operation Peace for Galilee.

Israel invades

Plans for such moves had existed for some time, but Israeli intentions were unclear. Officially, the operation was designed to push the PLO out of artillery/rocket range of Israel (about 40 km/25 miles), but the Israeli Minister of Defense, Ariel Sharon, was in favor of a much more permanent policy, involving an advance as far as Beirut and the complete military destruction of the PLO. In the event, Sharon's strategy prevailed, and

between June 6 and 11, the Israelis put into effect a stunning display of military skill.

The invasion was three-pronged. The main thrust was along the coast, with armored columns bypassing PLO camps at Tyre, Sidon and Damour and thrusting straight for the southern approaches to Beirut. PLO strongholds were left to follow up infantry units, some of whom landed by sea, although it proved less costly (to the Israelis) to stand off and destroy the camps using artillery.

Meanwhile two other columns had entered Lebanon from the area of Kiryat Shmona. One of these, spearheaded by the highly experienced Golani Brigade, took the Palestinian stronghold at Beaufort Castle (an old Crusader fort) and pushed across country to link up with the coastal column; the other, which included units of the new Israeli-produced Merkava tank, advanced north towards Lake Qaraoun to plug the base of the Beka'a Valley.

The problem of the SAMs was dealt with on June 9, when the Israelis used remotely-piloted vehicles (RPVs – unmanned small aircraft) to discover the precise location of the SAMs, as well as their radar frequencies, preparatory to highly successful air strikes. When the Syrians tried to intervene they were defeated – in the air by the Israeli Air Force (which downed a total of 84 Syrian aircraft for no loss to themselves), and on the ground by the Merkavas, which proved a match for the Soviet-supplied T-72s which appeared. By June 11, all of southern Lebabnon had been seized and the Israelis were beginning to probe the defenses of West Beirut, having trapped a Syrian brigade and many PLO fighters in the city.

Israeli problems

In normal circumstances, such a crushing blow would have been followed by superpower intervention, stopping the fighting before the Arabs could recover, but this did not happen in 1982, chiefly because the United States was far more concerned about what was taking place in the South Atlantic, where the Falklands War between Britain and Argentina was coming to an end. As a result, the Israelis were forced to keep fighting in the difficult built-up areas of West Beirut until late

August, when a ceasefire was negotiated. By then, the war had begun to fuel disquiet in Israel itself, particularly when it became apparent that little care had been taken about civilian casualties or the destruction of Lebanese towns.

The ceasefire agreement allowed the Syrians and PLO to withdraw from West Beirut, under the supervision of a special multinational force (MNF), composed of troops from the United States, Italy and France. The Palestinians were to leave all their heavy weapons behind and were to be dispersed throughout the Arab world. The evacuation went smoothly and, in early September, the MNF withdrew. As the Israelis pulled back to the outskirts of the city, it looked as if they had won a major victory.

Sabra and Shatilla

But nothing could be that straightforward in the maelstrom of Lebanon. The Israeli actions in West Beirut had resulted in most of the residents combining to oppose the invasion and siege, and although a new Lebanese government was about to be formed under the presidency of Bashir Gemayel, even that proved to be a prelude to disaster. On September 14, Bashir was killed in a car-bomb explosion. The Israelis, deter-

Civilians try to find a refuge from the fighting following the Israeli invasion of Lebanon, June 1982.

mined to disarm the Muslims in West Beirut, used the opportunity to send in massive forces.

Unfortunately, in the process, Christian militia units (possibly those under Saad Haddad), entered the Palestinian camps at Sabra and Shatilla, just to the north of the international airfield: for 24 hours they roamed the streets killing anyone they could find. An estimated 800 old men, women and children died. The international outcry was intense, forcing the Israelis (under whose command the Christian militias were supposed to be) to withdraw. An internal inquiry in Israel laid the blame for allowing the massacre to happen on Sharon and some commanders on the spot. Such criticism did nothing to reduce the opposition to the war in Israel itself.

The MNF returns

Later in September, Bashir Gemayel's brother Amin became the new president of Lebanon, and one of his first acts was to request the return of the MNF, this time to act as a buffer between the Muslim and Christian factions around Beirut. By October 1, US, Italian and French contingents had come ashore, establishing positions around the international airfield, the Palestinian camps and inside West Beirut respectively. They were joined by a small British contingent in February 1983, which patrolled an area to the east of the "Green Line" separating the warring factions.

This did nothing to stop the fighting. Indeed, as the MNF acted as a shield, Amin Gemayel used the opportunity to try to establish a firmer grip, ordering his army to detain Muslims in Beirut. All he succeeded in doing was to alienate most of the non-Christian factions, including the Druze, who began to attack government positions in the Chouf Hills. Meanwhile, Israeli forces further south were coming under increasing attack from Shi'ite groups resentful of the continued occupation.

Lebanon and Israel make peace

In an attempt to break the deadlock, the United States tried in the spring of 1983 to bring about the withdrawal of both Israeli and Syrian forces from Lebanon. On May 17, 1983, as a prelude to the Israeli withdrawal, peace was signed between her and Lebanon, ending the state of war which had existed for 35 years. However the Syrians, who had now been reequipped by the Soviets, refused to join the withdrawal and the whole process collapsed. President Assad, realizing that his support for the Muslims in

Lebanon could lead to increased Syrian influence, decided to bide his time. Hardly surprisingly, the Israelis refused to pull back while the Syrians remained in the Beka'a Valley.

The fighting intensifies

This did nothing to solve the problems facing Gemayel. In the summer of 1983 his army came under increasing attack from the Shi'ite Amal militia and the Druze, and in a desperate attempt to shore up his authority, the United States and France began to be drawn into the fighting. The US naval flotilla off the coast was reinforced by the battleship USS *New Jersey*, which began lobbing 16-inch shells into the Chouf Hills against Druze positions, while French and US aircraft flew combat missions over Beirut. Such an escalation of the war culminated on October 23, 1983, when Shi'ite terrorists drove truck-bombs into the headquarters occupied by US and French MNF contingents: as the dust cleared, 297 soldiers lay dead.

The situation in Lebanon deteriorated rapidly in the aftermath of these attacks. President Reagan tried to organize a peace conference in Geneva, but little of value was achieved. Instead, elements of Gemayel's army, recruited from among the Muslim population, began to desert, leaving him virtually isolated. In February 1984, the MNF withdrew, leaving Beirut at the mercy of the warring factions. In desperation, Gemayel turned to Syria for support.

Israeli withdrawal

Another peace conference was convened, this time in Lausanne (Switzerland), chaired by the Syrian foreign minister, but even he could achieve little. It was not until the Israelis indicated that they would be prepared to pull out of southern Lebanon that progress was underway. By 1984 the war in Lebanon had been draining both the manpower and the economy of Israel for two years, and although the overall casualty figure was not large (just over 600 dead), opposition to continued involvement had been growing. With inflation in Israel running at a reported 450 per cent a year, it was clearly time to get out.

But there were stumbling blocks. The Israeli intention was to hand over southern Lebanon as far north as the Litani River to the rebel Christian South Lebanese Army (SLA), an offshoot of Saad Haddad's militia. The danger here was that such a move would be certain to be opposed, not just by the local Muslims but by the reconstituted Lebanese Army.

In the end, a three-phase withdrawal was arranged. The first, which took place in February 1985, saw the Israelis withdraw from Sidon and the area south to the Litani. The Lebanese Army moved in and was generally welcomed, but Shi'ite militiamen attacked the Israelis as they pulled back. They retaliated by striking at the Shi'ite villages, but the Israelis also moved straight on to the second phase of the withdrawal, which was to vacate their zone of occupation adjoining the Syrian border. They took over 1,000 Shi'ite prisoners with them; something which merely intensified Shi'ite hatred.

The Beirut hijacking

The climax came in June 1985, when a US airliner was hijacked on a flight from Athens and forced to land at Beirut. One of the passengers, a US serviceman, was killed by the extremist Shi'ite terrorists and the lives of the rest were held forfeit against the immediate release of the Shi'ites in Israeli jails. Israel refused to trade, but a deal was clearly organized: the passengers were set free and, over the next three months, the Israelis released their prisoners in batches.

That same month, June 1985, the Israelis completed their withdrawal from Lebanon, although they left many "advisers" with the SLA in the border area. Israel also warned Syria against any attempt to fill the vacuum created by the withdrawal, even flying combat missions over the Beka'a Valley to ensure this. But Syria was playing a more subtle game.

Syria's policy

Assad wanted a stable Lebanon which could be an effective buffer against Israel. He saw the main threat to this as a resurgence of support for Yasser Arafat, which had occurred in the refugee camps since 1982. He also recognized the need for cooperation between the Muslims and Christians, and was prepared to back the Shi'ite and Druze militias in the belief that they could put pressure on the Christians to accept a reduction in their traditional political and social privileges. This had to happen if the Muslims were to have an equal share in the running of the country.

In order to crush pro-Arafat elements in the refugee camps, Assad encouraged the Shi'ite militias to attack them in May 1985. PLO resistance was stronger than expected, and only one out of the three camps in the Beirut area fell.

Life goes on at the Shatilla camp for Palestinian refugees, under attack from Shi'ite militias, June 1985.

The *Hezbollah*
A further problem was the presence of Iranian backed fundamentalist militias, especially the extremist Shi'ite *Hezbollah* (Party of God). In 1985 it embarked on a program of kidnaps of Western journalists and other civilians, hoping to use them as bargaining counters to secure the release of terrorists held in jails in both Europe and the Middle East.

The rise of *Hezbollah* and other extremist groups, the resurgence of the PLO in the refugee camps and Christian resistance to reforms brought increasing chaos to Lebanon in 1986. Fighting flared up again in Beirut, the Shi'ites continued to lay seige to the Palestinian refugee camps and *Hezbollah* kidnappings and attacks on the Israeli-backed SLA in the south all combined to make the country ungovernable.

In early 1987, the Syrians stepped in, sending troops onto the streets of Beirut to restore order. They did not succeed entirely, but the expansion of Syrian influence, achieved without causing an Israeli response, implied that Assad had just been waiting for the right moment. Whether that had now passed or whether this latest move was merely a prelude to a complete takeover of Lebanon and the reemergence of "Greater Syria" remained to be seen.

Prospects for peace
None of this did much to solve the basic problems of the Middle East, particularly the position of the Palestinians, but it would be wrong to suggest that the peace process was entirely dead. One of the most remarkable aspects of the recent history of the Middle East was the recovery of the PLO from its defeat in 1982 and its increasing role in the pursuit of a settlement favorable to the Palestinians.

The initial effect of the withdrawal from Beirut in September 1982 was to split the PLO into three parts. First there was Arafat at the head of *Fatah*, still prepared to negotiate for a solution to the Palestinian problem. In the middle stood a grouping, politically to the left, under George Habash (founder of the Popular Front for the Liberation of Palestine), which did not like the idea of negotiation but was not prepared to make a complete break with Arafat. Finally, there was the Syrian-backed Nationalist Alliance, which was vehemently against Arafat, even to the extent of fighting *Fatah* forces in northern Lebanon in 1983.

An element of order was restored in July 1984, when the Palestinian National Council (PNC) agreed to back Arafat's continued leadership of the cause, and he used this mandate to pursue the possibility of peace. By February 1985, he had joined with King Hussein of Jordan to put forward a new proposal.

The Hussein Plan
This called for an exchange of territory for peace within a framework which included all members of the UN Security Council as well as the countries and groups directly involved. It called for Palestinian self-determination in terms of confederation with Jordan and spoke of a joint Jordanian-Palestinian delegation at future peace talks. The overall aim was to give the West Bank and the Gaza Strip to the Palestinians as a "homeland," but under the control of the Jordanians and, hopefully, the Egyptians. It made no mention specifically of Resolution 242.

It did not work, however. Syria soon made it clear that she was opposed (Assad even dismissed Arafat's representative from Damascus); Israel refused to enter any negotiations with a team which included the PLO; the moderate Arab countries (with the exception of Egypt) were lukewarm and even the United States, recognizing that the plan would have to include the Soviets (as permanent members of the Security Council) in the peace process, refused to give it their full backing.

King Hussein spent a fruitless year (1986) trying desperately to gain support, during which it became clear that the PLO was intent on using Jordan as a launch pad for further attacks on Israel. By the end of the year, the King had decided to sever his links with the PLO and concentrate instead on more direct talks with Israel about the future of the West Bank, formerly part of Jordan. Once more, the peace process had foundered, but at least people were still prepared to try.

The future
With Lebanon still in chaos, Israel not yet fully secure and a bitter war raging in the Gulf, the Middle East continues to live up to its reputation as the most volatile region of the modern world. None of the tensions and problems which created this reputation has been tackled – the dilemma of the Palestinians remains, Israel still occupies Arab territory, religious differences proliferate and the superpowers continue to interfere whenever they feel threatened – and the future looks bleak. Many people in the Middle East have known nothing but war and violence, which have become a way of life. So long as the problems persist, this is likely to remain the case.

CONFLICT IN THE 20TH CENTURY: APPENDICES

The different countries of the Middle East reflect the full range of religious, ethnic and political divisions of the region. These have produced a succession of wars as well as a host of internal squabbles, best illustrated by the example of Lebanon, and this has given outside powers full opportunity to intervene, especially where oil supplies appear to be threatened. In such circumstances, Middle East leaders have to be particularly able if they are to survive.

PERSONALITIES

Hafez Assad (1928-   ) President of Syria. He was commissioned into the Syrian Air Force in 1955 and three years later trained in the Soviet Union. He opposed Syria's departure from the United Arab Republic in 1961 and was dismissed from the air force. A member of the Ba'ath Party, he soon became leader of the military wing. Following a power struggle within the Ba'ath Party, he became President of Syria in 1971. He has tried to improve relations with other Arab countries. This led to Syria's contribution to the 1973 Arab-Israeli war. In 1982, though, he turned against Iraq and now supports Iran. He has also fostered close ties with the Soviet Union. He rules Syria with firmness and uses repression to stamp out threats to his position. In 1982 he crushed the Muslim Brotherhood, with the loss of 10,000 lives.

David Ben-Gurion (1886-1973) First Prime Minister of Israel. He was born in Russia and emigrated to Palestine in 1906. He soon became politically active, forming the Workers of Zion Party. During the First World War he was arrested by the Turks for his Zionist activities but later joined the British-raised Jewish Legion. In 1930 he founded the *Mapai* or Workers' Party. He led the struggle against the British mandate and was made prime minister in 1948. Defeated in the 1953 elections, he was prime minister again and defense minister 1955-63. Apart from guiding the Jews through two wars and making

David Ben-Gurion

Hussein ibn Talal

Israel a viable independent state, his rule was characterized by a tough military policy towards Israel's enemies.

Amin Gemayel (1942-   ). Lebanese President. Elder son of Pierre Gemayel, founder of the Phalangist movement in Lebanon, Amin originally practiced as a lawyer before entering parliament in 1972. Very much more moderate than his brother Bashir, he did much to restore relative peace in the aftermath of the 1975-76 Lebanese Civil War. In 1982 he became President of Lebanon after his brother had been assassinated. His efforts to restore peace in troubled Lebanon have been largely frustrated by his lack of a strong power base and he is little more than a figurehead.

Hussein ibn Talal (1935-   ) King of Jordan. Educated in Britain, he succeeded to the throne in 1952, after his father had been deposed because of illness. His aim was to improve Jordan's economy and he relied heavily on Western aid to do this. This made him unpopular with the other Arab frontline states and there were attempts on his life. He has had problems with the PLO, who have tried to create a state within a state in Jordan. In 1979 he abandoned his pro-Western stance in favor of non-alignment.

Saddam at-Takriti Hussein (1937-   ) President of Iraq. He joined the Ba'ath Party at an early age and was exiled for a time as a result. He became President in 1979 and was determined that Iraq should take Egypt's place as the leading state of the Arab world. His self-confidence was shown in 1980 when he arranged the first elections in Iraq since 1958 and the Ba'athists retained power with a large majority. With the support of the people, he was able to attack Iran. The war, however, has reduced his prestige in the Arab world.

Ruhollah Khomeini (c1900-   ) Ayatollah and leader of Iran. He comes from a family of religious leaders. In the 1950s he became a major religious leader. His agitation against the Shah resulted in his being imprisoned in 1963 and then exiled to Iraq. He stayed there, gathering support, until he was ordered out of the country in 1978. By this time he had gained much support in Iran. A popular uprising resulted and Khomeini found himself in power. His policy of returning to traditional Islamic values has kept the majority of Iranians behind him, in spite of the high casualties of the war with Iraq. He has been determined to remove all traces of the Shah's rule and policies and has been ruthless with opposition.

Golda Meir (1898-1978) Prime Minister of Israel. Born in Kiev, Russia, her family emigrated to the United States in 1906. In 1921 she went to Palestine and by the 1930s had become the leading female Zionist politician. In 1948 she was appointed Minister to Moscow. In 1956 Ben-Gurion made her his foreign minister and she changed her name from Myerson to the Hebrew Meir. She was prime minister of Israel from 1969 until resigning in 1974. Her time in office was marked by much traveling abroad in order to put Israel's case to the world.

Mohammed Reza Pahlavi (1919-1980) Shah of Iran. He succeeded his father as Shah in 1941, after the British had exiled his father because of his pro-German sympathies. In 1953 he was forced to leave Iran for a short time after Mossadeq had seized power, but

Ruhollah Khomeini

quickly regained his throne with US help. He embarked on a program of wholesale modernization of Iran, which became known as the White Revolution. Gradually the Iranian people turned against him because of his corrupt and repressive regime. He was forced to leave the country in early 1979 and was eventually granted asylum by Egypt, where he died.

Qabus Bin Said (1940–) Sultan of Oman. Educated in Britain, he was summoned home by his autocratic father in 1965 and imprisoned for five years. By 1970 Oman was under threat from Marxist South Yemen and Qabus realized that the only way to save his country was to

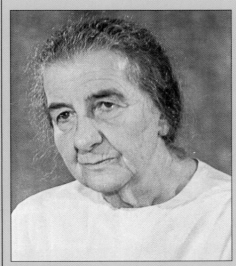

Golda Meir

improve the lot of the people. He staged a successful coup against his father. His modernization program and successful military campaign (coordinated by the British) resulted in victory over the Yemeni inspired insurgents in 1975. While he has done much to bring Oman into the 20th century, power is still concentrated in the hands of the Royal Family.

Mohammed Anwar el-Sadat (1918-1981) President of Egypt. Commissioned into the Egyptian Army in 1938, he was imprisoned by the British for a time during the Second World War because of his nationalist activities. In 1950 he joined Nasser's Free Officers' Committee. He served two terms as vice-president, 1964-66 and 1969-70, becoming president on Nasser's death. After the 1973 war he realized that the only way to achieve peace in the Middle East was to concede Israel's right to exist. This isolated Egypt from the rest of the Arab world, but in 1979 ended the 30 years' state of war between Egypt and Israel. He was awarded the Nobel Prize for Peace in 1978 for his efforts. Three years later, he was assassinated by Egyptian extremists.

Sheik Ahmed Zaki Yamani (1930-   ). Saudi Arabian Oil Minister. Educated at Cairo University and the Universities of New York and Harvard, he qualified and practiced as a lawyer. In 1962 he was appointed the Saudi Arabian Minister for Petroleum and Oil Resources and held this post until being removed in early 1987. He came to world prominence as Chairman of OAPEC in 1974-75 and was largely responsible for removing the 1973 oil embargo imposed on the West. His realism and moderation acted as a check for many years on the extremism of some OAPEC members.

Yasser Arafat *see Terrorism and Civil Strife*

Gamal Abdel Nasser *see Africa*

POLITICAL UPDATE

Bahrain
Capital: Manama
Population: 420,000
Constitution: Independent Sheikdom
Orientation: Member of Gulf Co-operation Council (GCC) and League of Arab States. Links with the West, treaty of friendship with Britain
Armed Forces: Army 2,300; Navy 300; Air Force 200

Egypt
Capital: Cairo
Population: 49.5 million
Constitution: Presidential republic
Orientation: Membership of League of Arab States suspended in 1979 after peace agreement with Israel. Now has closer links with West than Soviet Union, including arms co-operation agreements with Britain, France and United States
Armed Forces: Army 320,000; Navy 20,000; Air Force 25,000
Internal Opposition: Muslim Brotherhood (fundamentalist)

Iran
Capital: Tehran
Population: 45.2 million
Constitution: Revolutionary Islamic fundamentalist dictatorship
Orientation: At war with Iraq. Seeks to export Islamic fundamentalism throughout Middle East. Has no liking for either the United States and Western Europe or Soviet Union. Enjoys friendly relations with Libya and and Syria. Member of Organization of Petrol Exporting Countries (OPEC).
Armed Forces: Army 305,000; Revolutionary Guard Corps 350,000; Navy 14,500; Air Force 35,000
Internal Opposition: Exiled moderate Iranians and the Kurds

Iraq
Capital: Baghdad
Population: 15.4 million
Constitution: Socialist presidential republic
Orientation: member of League of Arab States and OPEC. At war with Iran. Enjoys passive support of most Middle East states, especially GCC. Soviet Union and Eastern Bloc has supplied her with arms for some years
Armed Forces: Army 800,000; Navy 5,000; Air Force 40,000
Internal Opposition: Kurds (2 million)

Israel
Capital: Jerusalem
Population: 4.4 million
Constitution: Parliamentary democracy with titular president
Orientation: Although at peace with Egypt, she remains in a state of war with her other Arab neighbors and has no Middle East allies. Has long relied on American support
Armed Forces: Army 112,000; Navy 9,000; Air Force 28,000
Internal Opposition: Palestinians living in the occupied territories

Jordan
Capital: Amman
Population: 2.7 million (excluding West Bank)
Constitution: Monarchy with elected parliament
Orientation: Member of League of Arab States. Traditionally looks to the West, especially Britain and United States
Armed Forces: Army 62,750; Navy 250; Air Force: 7,200
Internal Opposition: Occasionally from anti-monarchy, left-wing elements

Kuwait
Capital: Kuwait
Population: 1.71 million (including 1.1 million foreigners)
Constitution: Sheikdom
Orientation: Member of League of Arab States, GCC and OPEC. Traditional links with the West
Armed Forces: Army 10,000; Navy 1,100; Air Force 2,000

Iranian woman undergoes military training, 1980.

Lebanon
Capital: Beirut
Population: 2.6 million
Constitution: Presidential parliamentary democracy with seats tied to give equal Christian and Muslim representation
Orientation: Civil war since 1975 and occupied in part by both Israel and Syria, Lebanon has become a focal point for much of the region's problems, especially inter-Arab religious and political differences.The government now has little control over the situation. Syria wields the main influence, but Israel has some along the southern border areas
Armed Forces: Army 15,000; Navy 300; Air Force 300; Christian militias 5,000 active, 30,000 reservists; Muslim militias 4,000 active, 25,000 reservists
Internal Opposition: See appendix on religious groupings in Lebanon

Israeli APC during the Lebanese invasion, 1982.

Oman
Capital: Muscat
Population: 1.3 million
Constitution: Sultanate
Orientation: Member of League of Arab States and GCC. Has been given longstanding defense support by Britain and latterly by the United States
Armed Forces: Army 16,500; Navy 2,000; Air Force 3,000
Internal Threats: Periodic from South Yemen inspired guerrillas operating across the border

Qatar
Capital: Doha
Population: 300,000 (including foreigners)
Constitution: Emirate
Orientation: Member of League of Arab States, GCC and OPEC. Has treaty of friendship with Britain
Armed Forces: Army 5,000; Navy 700; Air Force 300

Saudi Arabia
Capital: Riyadh
Population: 11.6 million
Constitution: Kingdom
Orientation: Member of League of Arab States, GCC and OPEC. She relies largely on Western supplies of arms, but has no formal agreements with any state outside the Middle East
Armed Forces: Army 40,000; Navy 3,500; Air Force 14,000
Internal Opposition: Occasionally from fundamentalist elements

Syria
Capital: Damascus
Population: 11.25 million
Constitution: Presidential republic
Orientation: Member of League of Arab States. Has treaty of friendship and cooperation with the Soviet Union
Armed Forces: Army 320,000; Navy 2,500; Air Force 70,000

United Arab Emirates
Capital: Abu Dhabi
Population: 1.3 million (including foreigners)
Constitution: Federation of seven Sheikdoms (Abu Dhabi, Ajman, Dubai, Fujairah, Ras al-Khaimah, Sharjah, Umm al Qaiwain) under a President
Orientation: Member of GCC, League of Arab States and OPEC. Has treaty of friendship with Britain
Armed Forces: Army 40,000; Navy 1,500; Air Force 1,500

Yemen Arab Republic (North Yemen)
Capital: San'a
Population: 9.3 million
Constitution: Presidential republic
Orientation: Member of the League of Arab States. For some years there have been serious discussions with South Yemen over merging the two. Inclined to the Eastern Bloc
Armed Forces: Army 36,550; Navy 550; Air Force 1,000

People's Democratic Republic of Yemen (South Yemen)
Capital: Aden
Population: 2.3 million
Constitution: Marxist presidential republic
Orientation: Member of the League of Arab States. After earlier disputes has a closer relationship with North Yemen. Has close links with the Soviet Union, which is allowed to use the port and air facilities at Aden. Has made numerous attempts to undermine the Sultanate of Oman
Armed Forces: Army 24,000; Navy 1,000; Air Force 2,500

OIL

Since 1945 oil has been a crucial factor in Middle East politics. It was first discovered in Iran in 1908. Other sources were located in Iraq (1923), Bahrain (1932), Saudi Arabia (1937), Kuwait (1938), Qatar (1940), Abu Dhabi (1958), Oman (1963) and Dubai (1963).

Middle East output
Until the Second World War, the Middle East supplied only five per cent of the world's oil needs, but after 1945 this percentage rose sharply. Industrial development has radically increased demand and by 1965 the Middle East was supplying 25 per cent of world needs. Western Europe and Japan became almost totally reliant on Middle East oil and even the United States, which has extensive domestic sources, obtains almost half her oil imports from the region.

Control of oil
Originally oil production was wholly in the hands of Western oil companies, who obtained concessions from the countries concerned, but paid little for them. In 1950, Saudi Arabia, Kuwait and Iraq demanded a half share in the oil revenues and other countries followed suit.

The next major step was the 1972 General Agreement. Through this every oil-producing state was automatically entitled to a 25 per cent share in any concession. This was to rise to 51 per cent by 1982. Some states, notably Iraq, Iran, Kuwait and Qatar, have gone a step further and totally nationalized their oil.

OPEC is formed
Because oil was under-priced for so long on the world market, many of the oil-producing countries came together in 1960 to form the Organization of Petroleum Exporting Countries (OPEC). They included all the major Arab producers.

Initially, efforts to raise the price failed, but by 1970 demand was beginning to exceed supply. In 1971 an OPEC meeting in Tehran agreed that prices should rise in line with inflation.

The oil price jumps
In 1973 the Arab countries used oil as a weapon in order to weaken Western support for Israel. Prices were *quadrupled* overnight, which resulted in almost immediate recession for Western economies and mounting unemployment. Third World countries suffered more.

The industrialized nations quickly adapted to more expensive oil. At the same time differences grew within OPEC over prices. Radical states, like Iraq and Libya, demanded high increases, while more moderate countries, led by Saudi Arabia, wanted to restrain them.

Overproduction
A further problem arose over the rate of production. Prices could only be raised if this was cut back, ensuring that demand was greater than supply. OPEC found it increasingly difficult to regulate production by individual members and by the early 1980s there was a glut on the market, which forced prices to fall.

By this time, many of the oil-producing states had invested their huge revenues in ambitious widescale modernization programs. When prices began to fall they were put in the position of having over-reached themselves financially.

They were forced to accept that oil is a double-edged weapon. Unless carefully handled, there is a danger that it will rebound on its user. Furthermore, in recent years other sources of oil have been found, notably under the sea (offshore oil), which has made a number of countries less dependent on OPEC oil.

A meeting of the OPEC ministers, 1984.

OPEC MEMBERS

Algeria, Ecuador, Gabon, Indonesia, Iran, Iraq, Kuwait, Libya, Nigeria, Qatar, Saudi Arabia, United Arab Emirates, Venezuela

OIL PRODUCTION 1984

Oil production is usually measured in the number of barrels produced per day. A barrel represents 42 gallons (191 liters) of oil. Sometimes it is given in tons of oil (1 barrel = 0.136 of a ton).

Supertankers

The past 20 years have seen a new breed of ship transporting oil from the Middle East. These are the supertankers, the largest ships now afloat. Typical is the Japanese *Globtik Tokyo* which is 379m (415 yards) long and 62m (68 yards) wide.

This means that not only are they too large to use the ports and have to discharge their cargoes offshore, but also that they have to use the Cape route rather than the Suez Canal, thus decreasing its importance.

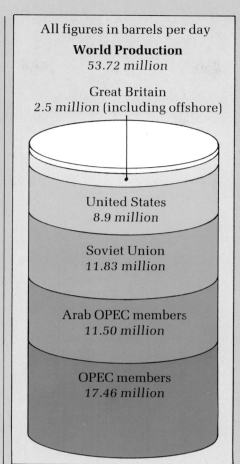

All figures in barrels per day
World Production
53.72 million

Great Britain
2.5 million (including offshore)

United States
8.9 million

Soviet Union
11.83 million

Arab OPEC members
11.50 million

OPEC members
17.46 million

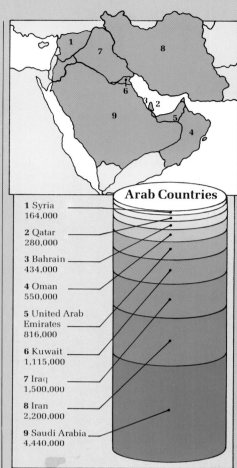

Arab Countries

1 Syria 164,000
2 Qatar 280,000
3 Bahrain 434,000
4 Oman 550,000
5 United Arab Emirates 816,000
6 Kuwait 1,115,000
7 Iraq 1,500,000
8 Iran 2,200,000
9 Saudi Arabia 4,440,000

The USS Stark *after being hit by missiles in the Gulf, 1987*

Shipping in the Gulf

The numerous attacks on merchant shipping in the Gulf have increasingly resulted in Western warships being sent there to escort national merchant vessels. In summer 1987 two events raised the danger of the Iran-Iraq War becoming more widespread. First, a US warship, the USS *Stark*, was badly damaged in error by an Iraqi fighter. At the same time, Kuwait, arranged for its tankers to be re-registered under the US flag so that US warships could escort them. This produces the possibility of direct confrontation between Iran and the United States.

SUMMARY OF CONFLICTS

Palestine, 1946-1947
The Jews resented British efforts to restrict immigration to Palestine, especially those who had suffered under Nazism in Europe. Illegal Jewish military organizations in Palestine, notably the *Haganah*, the extremist *Irgun* and the LEHI began to attack British military targets in the country. Terrorist incidents culminated in the blowing up of the King David Hotel in Jerusalem in July 1946 by the *Irgun*. Eventually, Britain handed her mandate over to the United Nations. Her troops left the country in May 1948.

Israel's War of Independence, 1948-49
With the declaration of Israel's independence in May 1948, she was simultaneously invaded by Egypt, Jordan, Iraq, Syria and Lebanon. Within two weeks much of Israel had been overrun. There was then a UN truce which lasted for a month, before Israel began a series of counterattacks to regain her lost territory. A second UN truce was implemented in mid-July 1948 and lasted until October. The final phase saw Israel consolidate her hold so that by early 1949 she had control of two-thirds of Palestine, as opposed to the 56 per cent allotted to her by the United Nations. Armistice agreements were signed between February and July 1949.

Arab-Israeli War, 1956
Stung by increasing guerrilla raids from the Gaza Strip and Sinai and an increasing Egyptian build-up, Israeli forces launched a surprise attack on Sinai on October 29. Within a week Israeli tanks had totally overrun the area and closed up to the Suez Canal. Vast amounts of equipment were captured. The Israelis also took some 6,000 Egyptian prisoners. A UN-imposed ceasefire then resulted in the Israeli forces withdrawing to their own borders by March 1957.

Suez, 1956
As a result of the nationalization of the Suez Canal Company by Nasser in July 1956, Britain and France decided to take military action. This was done in collusion with Israel. On October 31 British and French aircraft began a bombing campaign of Egyptian airfields. This was followed by paratroop operations against Ports Fuad and Said on November 5, and then landings from the sea. A UN ceasefire was quickly imposed and by the end of the year the Anglo-French forces had handed over to UN troops and withdrawn.

Yemen 1962-70
In September 1962, the Imam of Yemen died and was succeeded by his son. He was deposed by a coup led by Brigadier Abdullah Sallal. The Imam fled north to rally his supporters, while 30,000 Egyptian troops arrived to help Sallal. Royalist resistance proved spirited. In spite of being bombed from the air and gassed, the Royalists fought on gaining many local successes. The Egyptians withdrew after the 1967 Arab-Israeli war and Sallal was overthrown. Fighting continued, though, until Saudi Arabia organized peace in 1970.

Radfan and Aden 1963-67
Nasser helped the National Liberation Front in Yemen to try to drive the British out of Aden. Terrorist incidents began in 1963. In January 1964 the British launched a major operation designed to subdue the mountainous Radfan region north of the port of Aden. The aim was achieved by early June. At the end of 1964 there was a marked increase in terrorist incidents in Aden itself. The British counter-insurgency campaign lasted until November 1967, when their forces were withdrawn, handing the colony over to the NLF. It became independent as South Yemen.

Dhofar 1965-75
The rebel Dhofar Liberation Front, later absorbed by the Marxist Popular Front for the Liberation of the Occupied Arabian Gulf (PFLOAG), aimed to overthrow the Sultan of Oman. By 1970, almost all the Dhofar province bordering South Yemen was in PFLOAG hands. Qabus, the Sultan's son, overthrew his father and requested British-military help. Iran and Jordan also sent troops. In a masterly campaign the British-led forces succeeded in eventually clearing the Dhofar, although the threat from South Yemen remained.

Arab-Israeli War (Six-Day War) 1967
Believing that the frontline Arab states were preparing to attack her, Israel launched surprise strikes on June 5. She began with air attacks on Egyptian, Syrian and Jordanian airfields in order to achieve air supremacy and then launched land attacks on Sinai, Jerusalem and the Golan. By the end of the six days she had overrun the whole of Sinai, seized the Golan Heights and captured all Jordanian territory on the West Bank of the Jordan. She held on to this territory in order to provide a buffer against future Arab attacks on Israel.

War of Attrition 1969-70
The period March 1969 – August 1970, although not outright war, was marked by a number of raids and clashes between Israel and Egypt.

Arab-Israeli War (Yom Kippur War) 1973
Israel was taken by surprise when Egyptian forces crossed the Suez Canal and attacked the Bar Lev Line and Syria attacked the Golan Heights on October 6, the holiest day in the Jewish calendar. The Egyptians penetrated the Israeli defenses and inflicted heavy casualties, but halted behind anti-aircraft and anti-tank defenses. Israel was therefore able to deploy reinforcements and mount a counterstroke. On the night October 15/16 the Israelis crossed the Suez

Omani soldier guards the Darra Ridge in Dhofar, 1976.

Canal and began to threaten the Egyptian rear. In the north, too, the Syrians had early successes, but were pushed slowly back, even though they received Iraqi and Jordanian reinforcements. An overall ceasefire was eventually arranged on October 24, with Israel once more the victor, in spite of her early reverses.

Lebanon 1975-

Fighting between Christians and Muslims broke out in Tripoli in mid-March 1975 and spread to Beirut, where the PLO became involved. The Syrian Army moved in and occupied the Beka'a Valley. In October a ceasefire was arranged. Fighting broke out again between the Christians and PLO in February 1977.

In retaliation for PLO raids, Israel launched Operation Litani into southern Lebanon in March 1978, UN troops taking over on her withdrawal.

On June 6, 1982, Israeli forces invaded Lebanon a second time, clashing with both the PLO and Syrian forces. The PLO were forced to evacuate Beirut, but fighting between Christians and Muslims continued, especially in Beirut.

President Gemayel now invited the multinational force (MNF) of US and West European contingents to keep order in Beirut. The MNF was withdrawn in February 1984, having made no progress.

In January 1985 Israel began to withdraw from Lebanon, harried by the Muslim militias. The Lebanese Army tried to take over, but without success. During 1985 and 1986 Christians continued to fight Muslims; Shi'ite militiamen, supported by Syria, attacked the PLO, now back in the Palestinian refugee camps; and Sunni fought Shi'ite. Eventually, Syrian troops entered Beirut in February 1987. The violence was reduced, but did not end.

Iran-Iraq War 1980-

Iraqi troops invaded Iran at several points on September 22, 1980. Although they achieved tactical surprise and captured territory, they could not break the Iranian lines. Iran counterattacked and regained most of her lost territory.

A war of attrition then started. In July 1982 Iran launched the first of her "human wave" offensives undertaken by largely untrained volunteers. These continued until mid-1984. Since then the war has been marked by limited offensives on both sides.

Neutral oil tankers in the Arabian (Persian) Gulf have been consistently subjected to air attack, mainly Iraqi, and there have been mutual bombings and rocket attacks on cities. Iraq has also used poison gas. There appears to be no end to the war in sight, with each side trying to wear the other out.

PLO soldiers leave Tripoli, Lebanon in December 1983.

LEBANESE FACTIONS

The current situation in Lebanon is very complex, but reflects many of the tensions which exist in the Middle East. The root of this conflict is tension between Christian and Muslim, but in recent years these two groups have fragmented for both religious and political reasons.

Christians

The vast majority of Christians in Lebanon are known as Maronite Christians. They are called after St Maro, who died c410 AD. They originated from the Syrian church and believe that Christ only exists as a God and did not come down to Earth as a human being.

As a result, they were excommunicated by the Church of

A Christian Phalangist (right) and Israeli soldier, 1982.

Rome, but reestablished links as a result of the Maronites' help to the Crusaders in the 12th and 13th centuries. They have, however, retained their own liturgy and hierarchy. Other Christian sects include Greek Orthodox and Greek Catholic.

Until recent years Christians have made up just over half the Lebanese population and have had more political power. Now, mainly because of the influx of refugees, the Christians represent only one-third of the population.

The Lebanese Army used to reflect the Christian majority in the country, but the Christians have now organized their own unofficial armies or militias in order to protect their regional interests. The main groups are as follows:

Lebanese Forces or Phalangists
By far the largest of the Christian militias (4,500 regulars, 30,000 reservists), they were formed by hardline Maronite politicians in 1976 to coordinate a number of smaller militias in Beirut.

South Lebanese Army
Formed in 1975 by a Lebanese Army officer, Major Saad Haddad, from the inhabitants of villages along the Israeli border. It is armed and heavily supported by the Israelis. It has a strength of some 1,000 men.

Smaller militias include the Right-Wing Guardians of the Cedars and the pro-Syrian Marada Brigades (also known as the Zehorta Liberation Army).

Muslims

The Muslims first appeared in Lebanon in the 7th century AD, when their armies invaded the region. Much of the fighting in the Crusades took place in Lebanon. There are three Muslim sects who inhabit the country:

Sunnis
The largest and traditionally most powerful of the Muslim sects, the Sunnis represented 20 per cent of the population in the late 1970s. They are orthodox in their beliefs and, apart from Iran, are the governing sect in every Muslim country. They make up the merchant and farmers' classes and have always occupied a privileged position. In recent years they have lost power to the more militant Shi'ites and Druze. They have a number of small militias of which the largest is the Tripoli-based Islamic Unity movement or *Taweed* numbering some 1,000 men.

Shi'ites
In the 7th century AD there was a split among the followers of Islam. The majority, the Sunnis, held true to the belief that the first three Caliphs were legitimate heirs to the Prophet Mohammed. The Shi'ites believe that the fourth Caliph Ali is the true successor, and that the Imam or leader is descended from Ali and has absolute religious and secular power.

They have always lived in the rural areas and it has only been in the last 50 years or so that they have begun to settle in the towns and cities, creating Shi'ite slums. The current strife in Lebanon has given them the opportunity to seize power. The rise of fundamentalism in Iran has also been a spur.

Amal is the main Shi'ite militia. It has some 6,000 regulars and 10,000 reservists. *Amal* means "hope" in Arabic and was formed in 1975 by Musa Sadr to protect Shi'ite villages in southern Lebanon against Israeli attacks.

Sadr followed a pro-Syrian line, which was resented by the more left-wing members, and it was this that caused his disappearance on his return journey from visiting Colonel Gaddafi of Libya in August 1978. Blame for this was put on Libya. Eventually, in 1981, Nabih Berri became the leader and remains so today. *Amal* remains pro-Syrian.

There are a number of more extremist Shi'ite militias who have assumed the mantle of Iranian fundamentalism and are more concerned over Iran's fortunes in her war with Iraq. It is they who have been largely responsible for the kidnappings of Westerners in Beirut, the object being to hold them as bargaining counters.

The strongest of these militias is *Hezbollah* or The Party of God, with 1,000 members. Others are Islamic *Amal* and the Islamic Resistance Movement. These groups aim to establish a Fundamentalist Islamic state in Lebanon and have clashed with the mainstream Shi'ites, whose aims are more modest.

Druze are an offshoot of the Shi'ites and have a strong belief in reincarnation. They live in the mountainous parts of northern Lebanon and have always believed in military action rather than words. Fiercely independent, they have in their time fought the Syrians, Israelis and Lebanese Army. Currently they are allied to the Shi'ites.

The Palestinian Connection

In the 1970s the PLO in the Lebanon pursued the policy of a "state within a state." This made the organization unpopular with not just the Israelis, but also the Syrians (who wanted a stable Lebanon to be an effective buffer against Israel) and an increasing number of Lebanese.

The evacuation of the PLO from Beirut in 1982 was thus generally welcomed. However, members of Yasser Arafat's *Fatah*, the largest PLO grouping, then began to creep back into the refugee camps. The camps came under threat from both the Christian Phalangists and the Syrian-backed Shi'ite *Amal*. They are now under permanent siege by the Shi'ites.

The Syrians do, however, back a breakaway branch of *Fatah*, the Popular Front for the Liberation of Palestine-General Command (PFLP-GC). There are also a number of extreme left-wing Marxist-Leninist groups who believe that Palestine can only be recreated once the Arab world has turned socialist. They are George Habash's Popular Front for

A Shi'ite prisoner about to be released by the Israelis, 1985.

the Liberation of Palestine (PFLP), from which the PFLP-GC broke away, the Popular Democratic Front for the Liberation of Palestine (PDFLP), another offshoot from the PFLP, and the Popular Struggle Front (PSF), which broke off from the PDFLP.

The situation is further confused by the existence of smaller and more shadowy terrorist groups, notable among which is the Abu Nidal Faction. It is very involved with international terrorists and has gone as far as killing PLO leaders who are prepared to negotiate with Israel.

Druze fighters on parade in Beiteddin in 1984.

CHRONOLOGY

1945

October 31 Jewish insurgents begin attacks on British targets in Palestine

1946

April 20 Anglo-US Commission recommends admission of 100,000 Jews to Palestine from Europe

July 22 Jewish terrorists blow up the King David Hotel, Jerusalem

1947

February 14 Britain hands over Palestine mandate to UN

November 29 UN recommends partition of Palestine

1948

May 14 British withdrawal from Palestine completed; state of Israel declared

May 15 Israel's War of Independence begins as Arab League forces invade the new country

1949

February 24 Israel-Egypt armistice signed on Rhodes; armistices with other Arab states follow

1951

April 28 Dr Mossadeq seizes power in Iran

July 20 Assassination of King Abdullah of Jordan

1952

July 23 Free Officers' Committee seize power in Egypt

1953

August 19 Dr Mossadeq overthrown and Shah of Iran reinstated

1954

July 27 British agree to vacate the Canal Zone of Egypt

November 14 Naguib deposed as President of Egypt; replaced by Nasser

1955

September 27 Nasser signs arms deal with Czechoslovakia

1956

July 26 Nasser nationalizes the Suez Canal Company

October 29 Israel invades Sinai

November 5 Anglo-French forces land at Suez (ceasefire imposed November 6)

1957

March Israeli forces withdraw from Sinai and Gaza Strip

1958

February 1 United Arab Republic formed between Syria and Egypt

July 14 Murder of King Faisal of Iraq

July 15 US Marines land in Lebanon to support government in civil war

1960

September 24 OPEC formed

1961

July 1 British troops sent to Kuwait to protect it against Iraq

September 29 Syria leaves the United Arab Republic

1962

September 26 Sallal seizes power in Yemen precipitating civil war

1963

March Coup d'état in Syria brings Ba'ath Party to power

1964

May Formation of the PLO

1966

February 23 Extremist officers seize power in Syria

November 4 Egypt-Syria alliance signed

1967

May 19 Nasser demands UN withdrawal from Sinai

June 5-10 The Six-Day War: Israel seizes Sinai, the West Bank (including Jerusalem) and the Golan Heights

November 22 UN Security Council adopts Resolution 242

November 29 British withdrawal from Aden completed: People's Democratic Republic of Yemen formed

1968

July PLO hijack Israeli airliner to Algeria

1969

March 15 Israel completes Bar Lev Line, Suez Canal

March 21   War of Attrition between Israel and Egypt begins

1970

July   Qabus seizes power in Oman; initiates campaign against PFLOAG rebels in Dhofar

August 7   End of War of Attrition

September 17   King Hussein of Jordan attacks PLO – "Black September"

September 27   Nasser dies

1972

July 18   Sadat orders Soviet advisers to leave Egypt

September 5   PLO murder Israeli athletes at Munich Olympics

1973

October 6-24   The Yom Kippur War: Israel attacked by Egypt (in Sinai) and Syria (on Golan Heights)

October 25   OAPEC raises oil prices by 70 per cent and places oil embargo on United States

1974

March 18   OAPEC lifts oil embargo on United States

November 13   Yasser Arafat speaks at the UN

1975

March   King Faisal of Saudi Arabia assassinated; replaced by his brother Khalid

May 13   Civil war breaks out in Lebanon

June 13   Iran and Iraq sign Algiers Agreement

September 1   Egyptian-Israeli Accord on Sinai

1976

June 1   Syrian troops move into north Lebanon and Beka'a Valley

July 3   Israeli rescue of the Entebbe hostages

1977

November 19   President Sadat visits Israel

1978

June 6   Israeli forces invade southern Lebanon (Operation Litani)

September 17   Camp David framework for Egypt-Israel peace drawn up

1979

January 16   Shah leaves Iran for good; Ayatollah Khomeini takes power (early February)

March 26   Egypt-Israel peace treaty signed

November 4   US Embassy in Tehran stormed and hostages taken

1980

April 24   Failure of US hostage rescue operation to Tehran

September 22   Iraqi forces invade Iran

1981

February 4   Gulf Cooperation Council formed (Saudi Arabia, Kuwait, Qatar, Bahrain, UAE, Oman)

June 7   Israeli aircraft destroy Iraqi nuclear reactor, Baghdad

October 6   President Sadat assassinated

1982

April 25   Israeli evacuation of Sinai completed

June 6-11   Operation Peace for Galilee: Israel invades southern Lebanon

August 18   PLO evacuation of Beirut begins under MNF (US, French, Italian) supervision

September 16/17   Sabra and Shatilla massacres, Beirut

November 1   Iranian Offensive, Gulf War

1983

February   British contingent joins the MNF in Beirut

May 17   Peace signed between Lebanon and Israel, later abrogated by Lebanon

October 23   Fundamentalist bomb attacks on US and French MNF bases in Beirut cause heavy casualties

1984

February 25   MNF withdraws from Beirut

March 1   Iraqi aircraft damage Indian merchant ship in Persian Gulf, the first of many such attacks

1985

January 14   Israel decides to withdraw in three phases from Lebanon

February 11   Jordanian-PLO peace initiative

1987

February 22   Syrian troops move into Beirut

May 17   US frigate *Stark* hit by Iraqi missile in the Gulf

July 22   US-escorted convoy enters the Gulf

INDEX

Note: Numbers in bold refer to illustrations or maps

FURTHER READING

Akehurst, J, *We Won a War. The Campaign in Oman 1965-1975* (Michael Russell, Salisbury, 1982)

Bull, O, *War and Peace in the Middle East: the Experiences and Views of a UN Observer* (Leo Cooper, 1976)

Gattan, H, *Palestine, the Arabs and Israel: the Search for Justice* (Longmans, 1969)

Cobban, H, *The Palestinian Liberation Organisation* (Cambridge University Press, 1984)

Cobban, H, *The Making of Modern Lebanon* (Hutchinson, 1985)

El Azhary, M S (ed), *The Iran-Iraq War* (Croom Helm, 1984)

Glubb, General Sir J, *A Soldier with the Arabs* (Hodder and Stoughton, 1957)

Halliday, F, *Arabia without Sultans* (Penguins Books, 1974)

Hassan, Bin Talal, *Palestinian Self-Determination: a Study of the West Bank and Gaza Strip* (Quartet Books, 1981)

Herzog, C, *The Arab-Israeli Wars. War and Peace in the Middle East* (Vintage: Random House, 1983)

Hirst, D, *The Gun and the Olive Branch: the Roots of Violence in the Middle East* (Faber and Faber, 1977)

Hoveyda, F, *The Fall of the Shah* (Wyndam Books, 1980)

International Institute for Strategic Studies: 'Military Balance' and 'Strategic Survey' (annual publications)

Katz, S M and Russell, L E, *Armies in Lebanon 1982-84* (Osprey, 1985)

Laqueur, W and Rubin, B (ed), *The Israeli Arab Reader* (Penguin Books, 1984)

Lawless, R I, *The Middle East in the 20th Century* (Batsford, 1985)

McNaugher, T L, *Arms and Oil: US Military Strategy and the Persian Gulf* (Brookings Institute, Washington DC, 1985)

Mansfield, P, *The Arabs* (Pelican Books, revised edn., 1983)

Ovendale, R, *The Origins of the Arab-Israeli Wars* (Longmans, 1984)

Pimlott, J L (ed), *The Middle East Conflicts* (Orbis, 1983)

Riad, M, *The Struggle for Peace in the Middle East* (Quartet Books, 1981)

Sadat, Anwar el-, *In Search of Identity* (Harper & Row, 1978)

Schiff, Z and Ya'ari, E, *Israel's Lebanon War* (George Allen and Unwin, 1985)

Stephens, R, *Nasser* (Pelican Books, 1973)

Sterling, C, *The Terror Network* (HR&W, 1981)

Thomas, H, *The Suez Affair* (Pelican Books, 1970)

Tripp, C, (ed), *Regional Security in the Middle East* (St Martin's, 1984)

(NOTE: All publishers located in New York unless specified otherwise.)

ACKNOWLEDGMENTS

Contents page: Rex Features; page 7: BBC Hulton Picture Library; page 8: BBC Hulton; page 10: Photosource/Fox; page 11 (top): BBC Hulton; page 11 (bottom): BBC/Bettman Archives; page 13: BBC/Bettman Archives; page 14: BBC/Bettman Archives; page 17: Popperfoto; page 18: Popperfoto; page 21 (top): BBC Hulton; page 21 (bottom): Photosource/Keystone; page 23: BBC Hulton; page 26: Hutchison Library; page 29: Rex Features; page 30: Stern; page 33 (top): Christine Osbourne; page 33 (bottom): Rex Features; page 34: BBC Hulton; page 35: Frank Spooner Agency; page 36: Rex Features; page 37: Stern; page 38: Rex Features; page 39: Stern; page 40: Rex Features; Page 41: Rex Features; page 44: Stern; page 46: Rex Features; page 48 (top): BBC Hulton; page 48 (bottom): Rex Features; page 49 (top): BBC Hulton; page 49 (bottom): Popperfoto; page 50: Topham; page 51: Stern; page 52: Rex Features; page 53: Rex Features; page 55 (top): Christine Osbourne; page 55 (bottom): Rex Features; page 56: Associated Press; page 57 (top): Topham; page 57 (bottom): Popperfoto.

PRINTED IN BELGIUM BY

proost

INTERNATIONAL BOOK PRODUCTION